The Lye & Wollescote and Chapels

A Victorian Cemetery and its Notable Burials

Best wishes
Jean Weston
&
Marlene Price

Researched and written

by

Jean Weston and Marlene Price

WEST MIDLANDS
Historic Buildings Trust

www.wmhbt.org.uk

First Published in Great Britain by
West Midlands Historic Buildings Trust
Canal Street, Stourbridge DY8 4LU

April 2010

ISBN 978-0-9565041-0-4

Printed by The Birches Printers Ltd
Spectrum House, Leamore Lane, Walsall WS2 7DQ

CONTENTS

West Midlands Historic Buildings Trust

The Lye & Wollescote Cemetery and Chapels

FOREWORD

The purpose of a Foreword is to introduce the reasons behind production of the book and to mark its parameters.

This is a remarkable book, some twenty years in the making, through two generations of researchers, and published now by the West Midlands Historic Buildings Trust (WMHBT) with financial assistance from the 'Awards for All' scheme of the National Lottery. Publication is also intended to promote the ambitions of WMHBT to refurbish the Lye & Wollescote Cemetery Chapels building to a new sustainable use; following much consultation and support from Dudley Council and the Architectural Heritage Fund, a scheme has been approved to re-configure the building for use as offices. The Trust is now seeking interest from potential tenants to provide the confidence necessary for funders to support the cost of the repairs and fit-out.

As public consultations for the building conservation scheme have evolved, it has become apparent that the occupants of the cemetery are an integral part of the social history of the area, every one having a story to reveal; some relatively mundane, others quite remarkable, but all essential contributors to the rapid growth of this industrial town at the very heart of the Black Country.

By good fortune these stories were researched and recorded by Denys Brooks from about 1985 until his untimely death in 1997. By even greater fortune, or some divine guidance, two present-day enthusiasts, Jean Weston & Marlene Price, realised the importance of recording for posterity a period in The Lye's history of development and growth that can never be repeated and took it upon themselves to prepare the notes that now form the basis of this book.

Throughout the investigations by WMHBT for the Chapels conservation scheme, it has been realised how sensitive any change of use of the building is felt by local residents, particularly in view of the close proximity of the cemetery. This book, we hope, goes some way to demonstrate that history has dictated the close association of past generations with the building and that recognising their contribution to the history of the town is all part of the overall scheme. The majority of the sales revenue generated from this book will be used to assist with development costs of the scheme to refurbish the Chapels building.

The research of Jean and Marlene has been detailed and meticulous in giving accounts of the work and life of the town's citizens; each one a story in its own right, making for a fascinating read. At the same time there is relayed an appreciation of how much we owe to our predecessors, and the capturing of the social history of a bygone age.

Alan T Smith MBE
Chairman,
West Midlands Historic Buildings Trust.
February 2010

An Introduction to
The West Midlands Historic Buildings Trust

The West Midlands Historic Buildings Trust (WMHBT) is a registered charity, established in 1985, with specialists in the field of building conservation giving their time on a voluntary basis to serve as Trustees and funds coming from membership subscriptions. WMHBT's purpose is to safeguard buildings within the West Midlands that are of historical or architectural importance. Where this cannot be achieved by simply raising awareness to the issues, WMHBT will consider carrying out a conservation project itself. As a registered Building Preservation Trust, WMHBT is able to attract grants and low-cost loans to carry out the type of rescue scheme often necessary with 'Buildings at Risk' and in this way aims to cover the deficit in funding such projects.

Membership is open to anyone with an interest in safeguarding historic buildings. The WMHBT organises a range of activities, focused on the West Midlands, to both encourage new members and involve existing members. Activities include a regular newsletter; specialist talks, events and visits to historic buildings; arranging public access (as appropriate) to buildings before, during and after repair; commissioning and publishing research into historic buildings; encouraging the involvement of schools and colleges in conservation projects; and disseminating information via the WMHBT website (see www.wmhbt.org.uk).

The first WMHBT project was 19-20 High Street, Kinver, South Staffordshire, a timber-frame building listed grade II. In the Staffordshire volume of 'The Buildings of England' series, the late Nikolaus Pevsner states that in Kinver High Street the best houses are numbers 17-20. To have lost an important building within that range would have been a tragedy, but when the WMHBT took the building over it was in a dangerous condition, with parts close to collapse. By that stage no-one was prepared to take up the arrears of maintenance because it would have cost more than the market value to put it right. As a result of the WMHBT project, 19-20 High Street has been transformed into a comfortable four-bedroom home and is now occupied by new owners. The high standards of the work were recognised by two awards: "The Carpenters' Award" presented by English Heritage in recognition of "the sensitivity of approach and excellence of craftsmanship"; and a "mention" by the Civic Trust for its "worthy contribution to the community".

The second WMHBT project was the grade II listed office building built as a living showcase by the former Harris & Pearson Company, firebrick manufacturers, in Brettell Lane, Brierley Hill, West Midlands. The building had been unoccupied for 13 years and was in a derelict state when acquired by the WMHBT, with the costs of repair again being in excess of market value. Conservation building work to convert the building for modern-day use as commercial offices commenced in April 2004 and was completed in January 2005 (see www.harrisandpearson.info for more information). The building was duly sold on and has been returned to use as prestigious offices. The project was a regional finalist in the RICS Awards 2006, a national finalist in the Brick Awards 2006, and was awarded a "commendation" in the 2006 Civic Trust awards.

Both of the above projects were made possible by tremendous local community and local authority support and financial assistance from several sources, including primarily the Heritage Lottery Fund and the Architectural Heritage Fund.

WMHBT has three current projects: The Weaver's Cottages, Kidderminster (listed Grade II); Lye & Wollescote Cemetery Chapels building (listed grade II), and several derelict buildings (listed grade II* and grade II) on the site of the former Foster, Rastrick & Co foundry in Stourbridge (manufacturers of the first steam locomotive to run on rails in the USA).

PREFACE AND ACKNOWLEDGEMENTS

In September 1993 Denys Brooks, an avid local historian and a stalwart member of the Birmingham & Midland Society for Genealogy & Heraldry, gave an illustrated slide talk to the members of the Stourbridge Branch of that society at Old Swinford Hospital, the school founded by Thomas Foley in the mid-seventeenth century. It was a remarkably researched history of Lye told through the headstones of some of the town's former inhabitants and interesting characters who are now buried in The Lye & Wollescote Cemetery.

Denys Brooks died suddenly in January of 1997 and it was thought that the photographic slides he had used for his talk together with his hand-written manuscript had been lost. However, Pat Dunn, who collaborated with Denys on the first book of '*Lye in Old Postcards*', discovered the slides amongst his effects and they came into our possession. With the aid of the slides and Denys's hand-written notes, which later came to light at the school, the original talk was painstakingly reconstructed and since 2002 has been presented to a number of local groups and societies. Over the past seven years research has continued, and more of Lye & Wollescote's deceased inhabitants who are buried in the cemetery have been added to the original.

In early 2008 we came into contact with Alan Trevis-Smith MBE, Chairman of the West Midlands Historic Buildings Trust, and David Trevis-Smith its Project Director, who took a great interest in our research and suggested that it could be expanded to include the creation of the cemetery and chapels. This we undertook to do and this history of The Lye & Wollescote's Victorian cemetery came into being. Our grateful thanks go to Alan and David for their assistance and guidance in bringing about this publication.

We are indebted to Pat Dunn of Lye & Wollescote Historical Society for her invaluable assistance when the original talk on the Cemetery was presented at Christ Church Lye in 2002 and for her continued support with the present project. We would also like to thank staff at Stourbridge Library, especially the former Chief Librarian, David Hickman, for allowing us to photograph the 'Webster' chair (see Chapter 6).

Thanks are due also to staff at Dudley Local History & Archives; to Worcester County Record Office and to the Bereavement Services department of Dudley MBC for assisting in the location of graves. We are grateful to architect Andy Foster for providing us with a copy of his research notes on Lye & Wollescote.

We would also like to thank several people: Phil Lamb for providing information on Lieutenant Turner (see Chapter 8) and providing photographs of the Thiepval Memorial, Gareth Manning for his knowledge on arboreal matters, Michael Reuter for allowing us to copy his post-card of the cemetery, Shelagh Thompson who brought the gravestone of Titus Webb to our notice and Nick Weston for his help with scanning photographs.

We are most grateful to author and historian Nigel Perry for suggesting improvements to the manuscript and for highlighting any historical inaccuracies. Any other errors are our sole responsibility.

We recognize that the people featured in this book represent only a small proportion of the approximately 17,500 inhabitants of Lye & Wollescote interred in the cemetery since its opening in 1879. We have, however, endeavoured to portray a cross-section of the people who in various ways contributed to the history of the area, and apologise to those whose ancestors are not included in this publication.

Jean Weston & Marlene Price
2010

Dedicated to the memory of

DENYS BROOKS
(1921 - 1997)

Denys was passionate about his birthplace of The Lye and its history.
In addition to collaborating with Pat Dunn on the book *'Lye & Wollescote in Old Photographs'*, he
was a prolific writer of letters and articles about his home town.
He was described in his obituary in 1997 as 'Mr Lye' because he was a mine of
information about everything and everybody in the town.

INTRODUCTION

In the early seventeenth century The Lye consisted of some thirty to forty scattered cottages. At around the troubled time of the English Civil War, a community of impoverished squatters settled on an area of the Lord of the Manor's common land, which came to be known as Lye Waste, situated about half a mile east of the centre of the main hamlet of Lye. The levies raised by both sides in the Civil War impoverished many people, and with the vastly increased demand for iron products, many families used the coal and clay on The Waste to supply the armies and were allowed to stay there. They built their mud huts from the clay but their wild and lawless nature kept them isolated from the surrounding towns and villages.

Over the next century those early inhabitants began making nails as a domestic industry and by the nineteenth century the nail-making industry had expanded with many larger companies producing nails in Lye. However, as machine-made nails came into being in the 1830s, demand for hand-made nails declined, and other industries began to spring up particularly chain-making, brick-making and the production of hollowware. By the late nineteenth century Lye had become one of the most productive and successful towns in the Black Country. The men who pioneered those industries were largely from families with humble beginnings, men who had little or no education, but their initiative, diligence and perseverance contributed to the growth and prosperity of the town. By the early 1900s, the hollowware trade provided more work for families than any other industry in Lye, which became known as the 'bucket capital of the world'.

The first major religious influence in The Lye were the Nonconformists who opened the first Chapel on Lye Waste in 1805, followed by the Established Church in 1813 when Christ Church Lye was erected on a site between the two villages of The Lye and The Waste. This had the effect of drawing the two communities together but, in spite of this, rivalry existed between the two factions and at the time of the opening of The Lye & Wollescote Cemetery in 1879 there were serious divisions between Anglicans and Nonconformists which did not end with death.

The Lye has always taken two things very seriously – one is politics and the other is religion. Local politics certainly played an important part in Lye's history though it may come as a surprise to some to learn that Lye has produced three Members of Parliament, and a fourth Lye man was nominated the official Liberal party candidate to contest the seat held by Prime Minister Baldwin.

Regarding religion, at one time in The Lye you were either 'church' or 'chapel' and 'never the twain shall meet'. To talk of rivalry between the two factions is very much an understatement, as in the past there was what could be regarded as open hostility between the two. In 1886 the then Vicar of Lye hit the headlines when he announced his intention to preach at the local Congregational Church and was pilloried in the press, both locally and in newspapers as far away as Birmingham. Such was the uproar caused by his statement that the Bishop of Worcester eventually stepped in and the Lye vicar was forbidden to carry out his intention.

This rivalry was also clearly evident in the re-election of members of the Burial Board in May of 1877 when, at a meeting of the Board, a poll was demanded for the Church candidate, though the decision of those present at the meeting was greatly in favour of the three gentlemen put forward on behalf of the Nonconformists. The election, which caused much excitement in the town, took place at the Lye Temperance Hall between 1 p.m. and 7 p.m., with the Vicar of Christ Church, the Reverend R Fletcher, officiating as Presiding Officer.

By seven o'clock an immense crowd thronged the streets near the Hall and at every vantage point in anticipation of the results which were announced by Mr Fletcher both inside the Hall and on the balcony in front of it. The news that the three Nonconformist candidates had been re-elected and that the Church candidate had been thrown out was greeted with prolonged cheers from the majority of the assembled crowd.

The townships of The Lye and Wollescote abounded with men and women of religious fervour with an unshakeable loyalty to their particular 'church' or 'chapel'. Many memorable local preachers emerged from amongst its ranks with some who went on to a higher calling within the church. There were those also who devoted their lives to public service and to the health and well-being of the community and who, even today, are remembered by the more mature of Lye's inhabitants.

Lye had its share of 'larger than life' characters and personalities, some of whom have achieved almost legendary status and whose exploits have passed into the folk-lore of the town, and there were those whose historical connections spanned several centuries. Though the town had its triumphs it was not without its tragedies, drawing its people together in an outpouring of communal grief.

The creation and opening of The Lye & Wollescote Cemetery in 1879, a rival to that of its neighbour Stourbridge which opened the same year, would undoubtedly have been a source of tremendous pride to a community once described as 'Mud City'. The history of the growth of that community in the nineteenth and early twentieth century can be told through the headstones of some of those inhabitants who helped to make it one of the most productive and progressive towns in the Black Country.

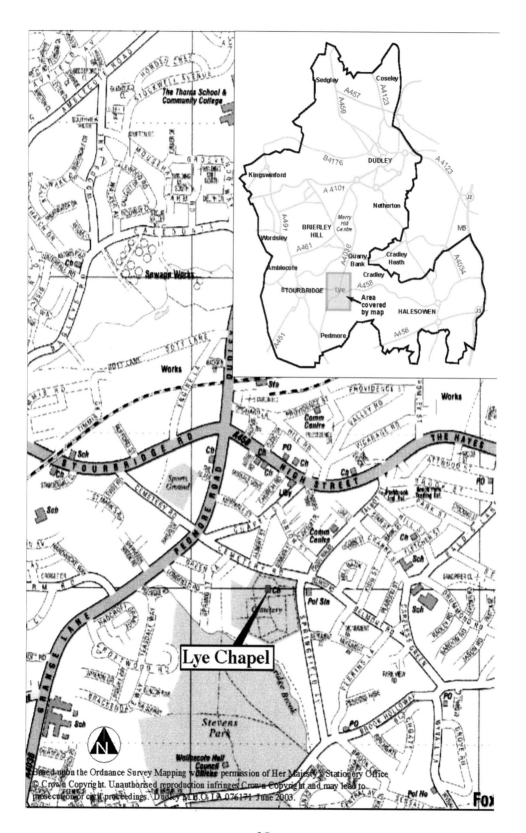

Lye Chapel

Chapter 1

THE EARLY HISTORY OF THE CEMETERY

The origins of the Victorian Cemetery

The emergence of the large cemetery was a major innovation of the nineteenth century. The Industrial Revolution had led to enormous population growth in urban areas and churchyards were filling up quickly. They were seen as unsanitary and unhygienic leading to the spread of disease. There was also a demand for providing a burial ground for other religious denominations within the community.

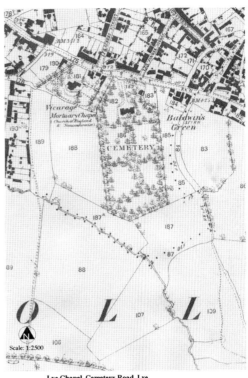

Lye Chapel, Cemetery Road, Lye
Ordnance Survey, First edition, 1882-1887, 1:2500

The earliest cemeteries in this country were created in the late eighteenth century but the creation of urban cemeteries, largely financed by private companies, grew in the early part of the nineteenth century and expanded rapidly during the reign of Queen Victoria. The earlier cemeteries were laid out in the style of a landscaped park with curving paths and shrubs and trees planted in scattered clumps. It was the publication in 1843 of *'On the Laying Out, Planting and Managing of Cemeteries'* by John Claudius Loudon (1783-1843) which had a great influence on cemetery design for the rest of the nineteenth century. He favoured a grid style pattern making the best and most efficient use of the available burial space and limited the planting of trees and shrubs to the edges of paths and driveways.

With a few exceptions Loudon's design followed the general plan of having a portal at the entrance to the cemetery combined with a gatekeeper's lodge. In a central or prominent position would be two chapels, one for Anglicans and one for Nonconformists which in some cases were linked by a porte cochere (a structure extending from the entrance of the building over the place where vehicles would pause to discharge passengers) and would carry a clock tower or turret. The chapels' buildings and the burial ground would be divided into two distinct halves, the western section used by Anglicans and the eastern section by Nonconformists; the Anglican half was consecrated ground. The Lye and Wollescote cemetery and associated buildings generally follow this classic layout including a clock tower but without a porte cochere.

The mid-nineteenth century saw a boom in the construction of public cemeteries by newly constituted publicly-financed Burial Boards. Burial Boards, appointed by parish vestries, were responsible for providing for the interment of the dead of the parish by building a cemetery funded from the poor rate. Public cemeteries were provided by Burial Boards until they became the responsibility of local authorities under Local Government Acts in the late nineteenth century.

The Lye and Wollescote Burial Board

In 1876 a group of nine local men formed a Burial Board and took on the responsibility for creating a cemetery for the parishes of The Lye and Wollescote. Among those men were a retired nail manufacture, a builder, a retired grocer, a brickmaker, a boot manufacturer and the manager of the local Co-operative Society. It is interesting to note that four of the men were Anglicans and five were Nonconformists. The first meeting of the newly-constituted Burial Board was held on Tuesday the 9th of May 1876 at the Lye Institution which became the permanent place of meeting at a rental of three pounds per annum inclusive of coals and gas.

Present at that first meeting were:

Stephen Albert Brooks	Samuel Moberley	Elisha Brooks
Thomas Mobberley	Isaiah Eveson	John Pearson
Thomas Hill	George Rhodes	John Hyrons

Stephen Albert Brooks was elected as the Board's first Chairman. He was the son of Joseph Brooks who lived at one time at 'Docker's Farm' and who, in around 1850, co-founded the partnership of Perry & Brooks with William Perry of the 'Vine Inn' in High Street, Lye. The firm made wrought iron products which included nails, chain, anvils and later frost cogs.

Elisha Brooks was elected as Vice-Chairman at that first meeting with Edward Westland Bernard, Solicitor of Pedmore, as clerk at a salary of twenty pounds per annum, and Mr Thomas, Manager of the Stourbridge & Kidderminster Bank, as Treasurer. Those officers having been appointed, the Burial Board could then set about its primary task, that of finding a suitable site for the location of the new cemetery and chapels.

A field called Doctor's Hill, part of the Old Swinford glebe, was considered to be a suitable and desirable site and an approach was made to the Reverend Henry Downing, Rector of Old Swinford, who expressed his inclination to sell this land. However, his patron and tenant, Henry Hickman, strongly objected to the proposal and the Board had to look elsewhere. Applications were then made to William Holcroft for land near the Grange called The Hopyard; to Thomas Bradley for land at Careless Green; to George Spencer Mathews, Steward to the Feoffees of Old Swinford Hospital, with regard to land at Oldnall and to Thomas Henry Pargeter of Wollescote House for part of Docker's Farm.

Messrs Holcroft, Bradley and Mathews all replied in the negative to the Board's applications but a letter dated July 31st 1876 was received from Mr Pargeter offering any portion of his land at Docker's Farm at the cost of £500 per acre. Negotations took place during the months of July and August between the Burial Board and Mr Pargeter who eventually accepted the Board's offer of £2,500 for the purchase of 7 acres and 22 perches of land, being part of Docker's Farm.

At a meeting of the Vestry held on 7th September 1876, chaired by the Reverend Robert Fletcher, vicar of Christ Church, the Board was authorised to contract for the purchase of Mr Pargeter's land at Docker's Farm for the sum of £2,500. The land was then in the tenancy of Joseph Perry, a nailmaster of Prospect House, Lye, son of the afore-mentioned William Perry. Joseph Perry was paid a sum of twenty pounds in compensation for relinquishing possession of the land. (Later he accepted, for the sum of ten pounds, the offer of the use of the land until it was required by the Board).

Authorisation was also given at the Vestry Meeting for the Board to borrow a sum of money - not exceeding £7,000 - for providing and laying out a burial ground and for building a chapel or chapels, which sum would be charged on the future poor rates of the parishes of The Lye and Wollescote. Having received this approval, William Fiddian was offered and accepted the post of Land Surveyor to the Board, and was instructed to prepare the necessary plans and reports.

At a meeting of the Board held in December of 1876 it was reported that approvals had been received from the Secretary of State to the suitability of the site, and from Her Majesty's Treasury for the Board to borrow the sum of £7,000. At that same meeting the question of the building of the chapels arose. It had been resolved to erect two chapels (as a single building), one for the burial service of members of the Church of England and one for the burial service of the non-members of the Church of England, in other words the Nonconformists. However, an amendment was proposed by John Pearson, seconded by Isaiah Eveson that one chapel only should be erected, but when put to a vote the original resolution to erect two chapels was carried.

At the start of the New Year of 1877 it was reported at a meeting of the Board that twenty-two replies had been received in response to advertisements inserted in 'The Architect', 'The Birmingham Daily Post', and the 'Brierley Hill Advertiser' for the submission of plans for the proposed new chapels. After consideration by the Board the plans of Thomas Robinson, Architect, of Stourbridge, were accepted provided they could be carried out for the sum of £2,500. At the same time, the Atlas Fire & Life Insurance Company had agreed to loan the sum of £6,000 for a term of 30 years at 4.1/4% interest. By the end of April, Thomas Robinson's plans had been sent to the Bishop of Worcester for his approval and a Mortgage was signed and sealed for the borrowing of the agreed sum from the Atlas Fire & Life Insurance Company.

At a meeting of the Board held on May Day it was reported that tenders for erecting the cemetery buildings had been received from five local contractors. It was resolved that the lowest tender, that of Isaac P Bloomer in the sum of £2,975, be accepted with the terms that he provide a bond with two sureties for the execution of the works or that £500 be left in the hands of the Board until after completion of the works. Mr Bloomer subsequently rejected those terms.

It was then resolved that the architect should consider what alterations and deductions could be made in the plans and specifications to bring the whole cost within £2,500. At a meeting held on 24th May, Thomas Robinson submitted his list of deductions, which included reducing the cost of erecting the lodge to £300, bringing the whole cost to a sum not exceeding £2,459. The amended Bills of Quantities in accordance with those deductions were sent out to contractors and eventually the tender of Mr C A Horton, builder of Brettell Lane, Kingswinford was accepted for the erection of the chapels, lodge and walls, amounting to a total of £2,421 10s 0d. He agreed to provide a bond with two sureties in the sum of £250 instead of the original £500 and fixed the date of completion of the works as the 1st of August 1878. The Board, however, objected to this date and, despite Mr Horton's insistence, it was resolved that the work should finish by the 24th of June.

With everything now in place it seemed that a year and a half after that first meeting of the Burial Board in May of 1876, work could at last begin on the creation of The Lye & Wollescote Cemetery and Chapels. The clerk was instructed to have a Board printed and fixed on the ground warning that 'Trespassers would be prosecuted'.

The Creation of the Cemetery

By September of 1877 work on the construction of the cemetery chapels was well under way. The first problem arose in mid-October when the architect and the builder advised the Board of the suitability of substituting a brick and stone spire for the slate one which had been originally specified. The architect produced a plan of the proposed new spire and the builder had prepared an estimate showing that he could complete the alteration for the sum of £69. The Board, however, failed to reach a decision on this proposal and it was left in abeyance for another meeting.

The Board found themselves with other more pressing matters to deal with, as it had been discovered that the rates levied by the Board on the Wollescote Township were double the amount of those levied on The Lye Township. At a meeting held on the 22nd November, a statement was issued to the effect that, though it was through no fault of the Board, it regretted the mistake and pledged that the irregularity would be rectified and in future an equal rate would be levied.

It was at the meeting held on the 29th November that the Board turned its attention to the materials which should be used to build the spire, but resolved to adhere to the original plan regarding its construction and refused to sanction any additional outlay. However, five months later in April of 1878 this decision was rescinded and it was agreed that the spire should be constructed in bricks instead of slate at an additional cost of £18 10s 0d.

John Mee, a nurseryman of Lower Mitton, Stourport was requested by the Board to prepare and submit for approval a plan for laying out and planting the cemetery ground for which he was paid the sum of ten pounds. Mr Mee's plans were accepted and at the beginning of January 1878 an advertisement for tenders for the work was placed in the local newspapers, one of those tenders being that of John Mee himself. His tender to lay out, drain and plant the cemetery ground for the sum of £500 was accepted by the Board and an agreement was drawn up which included the condition that he keep the ground, trees and plants in good order until the 29th of September 1878 and within two years of that date to replace all trees which may have died. This condition was later amended to one year.

Work on the chapels continued apace during the months of May, June and July of 1878 with only minor alterations to the original specification needing to be made. It was decided to dispense with the proposed terrace steps at the rear of the chapels and to turf the ground instead. An alteration was made to the entrance at an extra cost of £76 12s 0d and it was resolved that a lightning conductor should be fixed to the spire at a cost of five pounds or thereabouts. The surplus land was measured up and apportioned into garden allotments to be let in ten lots at one pound per lot per year. A cart road would be provided through the first lot and a barrow road through the next lots and an agreement made between the Board and the tenants that they, the tenants, would properly cultivate the land and keep the fences in good repair.

All appeared to be progressing well but by September the date agreed with the builder for finishing the work was well past At a meeting held on the 3rd September it was resolved that the clerk should write to Mr Horton complaining of the delay and informing him that it was intended to enforce the penalty for non-completion. John Mee, the nurseryman, attended that meeting and complained that in consequence of the builder's delay he was not able to proceed with his work and asked for a further fifty pounds on account. The Board, however, resolved to pay him ten pounds only.

As autumn approached the Burial Board turned its attention to the important matter of the division of the cemetery ground for Anglican burials and for those of the Nonconformists. The minutes record that at a meeting held on the 1st of October it was *resolved that the ground to the left of an imaginary line to be drawn from the middle of the boundary wall in front of the chapels to the centre of the boundary wall at the back be appropriated to the dissenters and that to the right of that line be appropriated for consecration'.*

William Fiddian's tender for laying out the burial ground in grave spaces at a total cost of ten guineas was accepted and his plan of the layout was approved subject to the provision of space being set aside for the interment of still-born children.

At the start of October 1878 an advertisement was placed in the local newspaper for the office of Sexton. Thirty three applications were received with the ages of the applicants ranging from twenty-three years upwards. The decision was put to a vote and Thomas Robinson of Birch Coppice, Lye (not to be confused with the architect Thomas Robinson) was elected as Sexton at a weekly salary of one pound plus free house rent. At sixty years of age he was the oldest of the applicants and in the years that followed the Board would have cause perhaps to regret their choice.

With the building of the chapels now complete, the laying out of the cemetery under way and a Sexton appointed, the Board must have felt confident that they were nearing the end of their initial objective. Before that objective could be reached, however, there was a further problem to be overcome – that of the nurseryman, John Mee. The Board was concerned that the work was not proceeding satisfactorily and he had not yet completed his contract. On the 30th of November a notice was affixed to the front door of the chapel which read as follows:

To Mr John Mee of Stourport in the County of Worcester

The Lye & Wollescote Burial Board hereby give you notice that on the expiration of seven days from the affixing of this notice on the Cemetery of the said Board, the said Board will in consequence of your delay proceed to complete the works still requiring completion in accordance with the contract entered into between you and the said Board and dated the 2nd day of February 1878.

Despite this notice Mr Mee failed to complete his contract and in January of 1879 the Board received a letter from him to the effect that he had petitioned for liquidation of his affairs by arrangement. It was considered whether to take legal action to determine the contract but in February it was resolved to employ somebody else to carry out the work still requiring completion.

With work almost finished, the clerk applied to the Bishop of Worcester to name a day for consecrating the Anglican portion of the cemetery and chapel set aside for that purpose and a day in early April was suggested. A reply was received from the Bishop's secretary to the effect that the date of the 18th April at 2.30 p.m. would suit his Lordship for the consecration of the Anglican portion of the cemetery. Mr Parker on behalf of The Lye & Wollescote Nonconformist Association had written to the Board requesting permission to perform a dedicatory service in the Nonconformist portion of the cemetery and this was agreed. It seemed all was now in place and the time was fast approaching when those stalwart members of the Lye & Wollescote Burial Board would see their aims fully realised. The new Sexton was instructed to take up residence in the cemetery cottage to await further instructions.

However, at almost the eleventh hour, a small problem arose. The clerk had been instructed to order a bell with a cross bar and wheel from Messrs Martineau & Smith at a cost of six pounds. On the 4th of March the clerk reported that he had casually informed the architect of the size of the bell which had been ordered, to which Thomas Robinson had remarked that the bell was much too small. It was, therefore, suggested that an advertisement be inserted in the *Daily Post* asking for estimates for a larger bell, which was subsequently ordered from Messrs Vickers at a cost of £29 6s 4d. All was now in place for the consecration ceremony.

Weather vane on Chapels' spire

The Consecration of the Cemetery and Chapels

The formal opening of the cemetery took place on Monday the 14th April 1879 and the following Friday was fixed by the Bishop of Worcester for the consecration of the portion of the burial ground allotted to the Church of England. The ceremony, however, did not go according to plan. A form of application had been received by the Burial Board from the Bishop, to be signed and returned, but the form was couched in terms to which the majority of the members of the Board, who were Nonconformists, objected. A resolution was passed to this effect which the clerk duly telegraphed to the Bishop who, in spite of this action, was prepared to go ahead and perform the ceremony on the appointed day.

On Friday the 18th of April a great crowd of people assembled at the burial ground to witness the consecration ceremony, among them the clergy of the Church of England, the architect Thomas Robinson, and a large number of local clergymen and notable gentlemen of The Lye. However, disappointment loomed as a little before three o'clock the Bishop's secretary arrived to say that His Lordship was not coming.

It appeared that the signature of the Secretary of State had not been obtained to a plan showing the division of the ground between the Anglicans and Nonconformists. This signature was necessary and the consecration ceremony could not be performed without it. Consequently, and no doubt with some embarrassment, the assembled dignitaries and the crowd were forced to disperse and the ceremony was postponed indefinitely. There was no such delay for the Nonconformists who went ahead with a dedicatory service in their chapel on the following Monday the 21st of April as a formal opening of their portion of the burial ground. The following day the first recorded burial took place in cemetery: that of Stephen Brookes, an infant of one month from Dark Lane, Lye, who was, of course, buried in unconsecrated ground.

Four weeks after the postponement of the first ceremony, the Church of England section of the cemetery was finally consecrated by the Bishop of Worcester on Monday the 19th of May. The unfortunate circumstances which had prevented the first ceremony taking place and the disappointment caused to the people assembled on that occasion had, it seems, caused considerable ill-feeling in the town with harsh words being directed, even against the Bishop himself. Consequently, the consecration ceremony which took place on that Monday was shrouded in secrecy in order to prevent any kind of disturbance. Though several policemen were stationed at the cemetery, their services were not required as only a comparatively small number of people gathered. The ceremony was witnessed by the members of the Burial Board and ministers of the local religious denominations. The Bishop expressed himself *'pleased with the arrangement of the cemetery and the handsome design of the chapels'*. Mr Thomas Robinson, the Bishop said, *'had succeeded in adding a pretty feature to the landscape of the vicinity'*.

Thomas Robinson, the Architect

Thomas Robinson, son of a spade maker, was born in Wollaston, Stourbridge in 1853. At the age of fourteen he entered the office of Thomas Smith, a local architect and surveyor in Hagley Road, Stourbridge, where Thomas acquired his knowledge and experience until Mr Smith died in 1876. Whilst still in his early twenties, Thomas Robinson took over the work on which Mr Smith was engaged which included additions to Enville Hall for the Earl of Stamford & Warrington, and St Mark's Church, Stambermill. His design for The Lye & Wollescote Cemetery Chapels was possibly one of his first commissions. Later in his career he was chosen, by competition, as the architect of Stourbridge Town Hall, erected by public subscription to commemorate the Jubilee of Queen Victoria and opened in November of 1887.

Subsequently he became architect to Kingswinford School Board whose area covered Brierley Hill, Quarry Bank, Brockmoor, Pensnett, Kingswinford and Wordsley and was responsible for the erection and extension of many of the schools built by the Board. When, in the early 1890s, John Corbett purchased Hill House, Amblecote and vested it in trustees as a hospital for the district, the necessary alterations and adaptations of the building were entrusted to Thomas Robinson. Among his other notable works were the chancel of Quarry Bank Church, a row of buildings in Stourbridge called Church Street Chambers and many Pedmore residences. He is believed also to have been the designer of a church built at Durham for the Cochrane family.

Thomas Robinson's distinctive architectural style is reflected perhaps in his love of locally-made red bricks used for both Stourbridge Town Hall and The Lye & Wollescote Cemetery Chapels, which together with his other work still in existence are a lasting memorial to this locally born architect. He never married and died on 9th June 1932 at his home at No 7 Red Hill, Stourbridge, aged 79 years, and was buried in Section E at Stourbridge Cemetery.

The Architecture of the Chapels

Access to the chapels is from Cemetery Road, through a set of wrought iron gates carried by gate pillars composed of alternate courses of red brick and limestone with elaborately carved copings. The gateposts and boundary wall are contemporary in date with the chapels building and superintendent's house and all are constructed in the Gothic style. The rather handsome chapels building is a perfectly symmetrical structure and is 'H' shaped in plan. It is constructed in red and blue bricks with limestone used for window and detailed ornamentation. The plinth is constructed in several courses of blue brick followed by a course of limestone, with red brick used for the main bulk of the building. The windows are of limestone tracery arched design with limestone hood moulds and are either two-centred or four-centred, apart from two 'wheel' windows located in the south-facing gable ends of the two chapels, above arched doorways giving access to the cemetery. Plain clay tiles have been used for the roof and are laid in decorative bands of plain and fish-scale tiles. The central octagonal spire constructed in yellow engineering bricks terminates in a weather vane bearing the date '1878'. The clock was installed in 1912 by A. Webb Limited of Lye to celebrate the coronation of King George V.

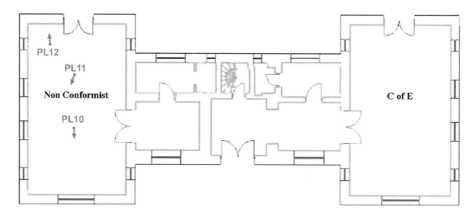

Lye Chapel, Ground Floor Plan of Chapels.

Located beneath the west chapel is a barrel-vaulted cellar which possibly functioned as a mortuary, with access being obtained externally from the south side of the building down a set of narrow steps.

The interior of both chapels have hammer beam roofs with lateral iron ties spanning between the upper sets of hammer-posts, with plaster inscribed in imitation of ashlar blocks. The windows have stained glass patterns and both chapels have polychromatic encaustic tiled floors, as do the entrance lobbies and passageways. A stone staircase leads up to the clock and belfry.

Originally the cemetery covered around seven acres and now extends to over nine acres. It is pleasantly situated on the Clent side of Lye and at the time of its creation was considered 'at not too great a distance for the convenience of funerals'.

Unveiling the cemetery clock, 1912. The clock was installed by A. Webb Ltd of Lye to celebrate the coronation of King George V. The photograph includes members and officials of the Lye Urban District Council. Back row, left to right: Councillor W. Chance, Councillor Perry, Mr Pugh the jeweller, Councillor Harrison, Mr H. Poole (sanitary inspector), Third row: Councillor B. Pritchard, Councillor A.H. Gauden, Mr Hart (Salvation Army) and Mr F. Hill (schoolmaster). Second row: Mr Basterfield. Mr Powell (sexton), Councillor Entwhistle, Mr W. Green (rates officer), Major Pardoe, Headmaster of Crabbe Street School and Mr H Folkes (surveyor). Front row: Mr S. Mobberly (clerk), Councillor Amos Perrins, Mr Watson Smith, who unveiled the clock, and Councillor D. Croft.

Chapter 2

A TALE OF TWO SEXTONS

The division that existed between the Anglican and Nonconformist factions extended also, it would appear, into the business of grave digging. This tale of two Sextons is perhaps one of the most bizarre, and at times comical, stories to have emerged from the history of The Lye & Wollescote Cemetery.

Thomas Robinson and William Pearson were both born in Lye in the year of 1812. Given that the population of the Lye in the early to mid-nineteenth century was relatively small, there is every possibility that these two men would have known each other. Their paths would certainly cross in later years and with Robinson being a 'chapel' man, and Pearson allied to 'church', doubtless there would have been a strong element of personal rivalry between them.

Thomas Robinson lived in Mears Coppice, Lye. In October of 1878 when the Burial Board advertised for a Sexton for its new cemetery, Thomas Robinson was one of the thirty-three applicants for the position. Grave digging was an arduous occupation; digging a hole six feet deep in any soil was not an easy task but with a salary of one pound per week plus rent free accommodation in the new cemetery lodge, often referred to as 'the cottage', it was obvious from the number of applicants that it was regarded as a job worth having, being both lucrative and long-term.

Thomas Robinson had formerly been occupied as a clay miner and a gardener so could be said to possess some of the necessary qualifications for the job, though at sixty years of age he was the oldest applicant. The job of a gravedigger was seen traditionally as a job for older men and the Burial Board appear to have carried on this tradition in electing to employ Thomas Robinson as their Sexton. It later came to light that he had not been completely truthful about his age and was, in fact, five years older than he had claimed at the time of his appointment. By the end of October of 1879 Thomas Robinson's wife, Eliza, also became employed by the Board to clean the chapels for which she was paid 11s 3d per quarter.

William Pearson lived in High Street, Lye. During his early working life he had been a nail maker and later a post messenger but in the mid-1870s he was employed as Sexton at Christ Church. In May of 1879, before a single grave had been dug in the consecrated section of the newly opened cemetery, William Pearson was at variance with the Burial Board. It seems that this dispute was related to the fact that, as Sexton of Christ Church, he claimed to be entitled to dig graves in the Anglican half of the cemetery for which he expected to be paid his usual fees. At a meeting of the Board on the 6th of May 1879, it was resolved that no fees should be paid to William Pearson until his claim had been substantiated. This situation was complicated by the fact that William Pearson's son, John Pearson, had not only been a member of the Burial Board since its formation but had recently been elected as its Chairman, and continued as Chairman for the next four consecutive years.

While this dispute between the Board and William Pearson was simmering, Sexton Robinson expressed the first of what would be many grievances in the years to come when he complained to the clerk about the conduct exhibited towards him by Samuel Rhodes on his being requested to remove his dog from the cemetery grounds. At a meeting held on the 9th of July it was resolved that the clerk should write to Mr Rhodes on the subject and inform him that any repetition of such conduct would result in proceedings being taken against him.

Cemetery Lodge

In September the Board received a letter from William Pearson, again claiming the fees arising from the graves which had been dug in the consecrated portion of the cemetery. The clerk, then Edward Treleaven, was instructed to acknowledge receipt of Pearson's letter but consideration of its contents was adjourned to the meeting held on the 14th of October at which it was resolved unanimously that the Board would not entertain Pearson's claim.

William Pearson took umbrage at this decision and in November a letter was received from his solicitors, Messrs Stokes & Harper, referring to the claim. The clerk was instructed to reply to the letter stating that the Board did not consider that Mr Pearson had any legal claim to such fees but that further enquiries would be made. Letters were sent to the Reverend Fletcher, Vicar of Christ Church, and to the former incumbent, Reverend Robertson, enquiring as to when, by whom and on what terms William Pearson had been appointed as Sexton at Christ Church and whether they considered him liable to be discharged and by whom.

The contents of the replies from the two Reverend gentlemen are unknown but were such for the Board to vote on the matter and to instruct the clerk to write to Messrs Stokes & Harper reiterating that they did not admit to William Pearson's claim. However, the Chairman of the Board, John Pearson, as would have been expected, abstained from voting and was supported in this by John Hyrons Hopes must have been high among the other members of the Board that they had seen the end of the matter.

In the meantime, by the start of 1880, Sexton Robinson was already finding that the work in the cemetery was becoming too much for him. Early in February he appeared before the Board to inform them that the pruning of trees, and other work requiring his attention, was much in arrear in consequence of his time being taken up by the number of funerals. He was also being plagued by children playing in the cemetery. Thomas Robinson was instructed by the Board to employ what additional labour he felt necessary and it was resolved that children under the age of ten years were not to be admitted to the cemetery except when under the control of an adult person.

In early March Sexton Robinson appeared again before the Board complaining of the behaviour of people visiting the cemetery during the past month. This complaint however, may have been used by him as an opportunity to acquaint members of the Board with the fact that the chimneys of his cottage were smoking very badly. It was resolved that an inspection of the chimneys would be made and the problem remedied.

Meanwhile, the Board's attention was again focused on William Pearson when, at a meeting held on the 15th of March of 1880, the clerk produced a County Court summons which had been served on him at the suit of William Pearson. It was resolved that Mr Perry of Messrs Freer & Perry, Solicitors of High Street, Stourbridge, should be consulted on the subject.

Meanwhile in early May, Thomas Robinson appeared before the Board yet again to complain about the number of small children visiting the cemetery and also the smoky state of his house. Both of these problems were clearly causing him some distress as he asked the Board to allow him two or three days' holiday in Whit week. It was resolved that a notice board be erected informing the public that children under the age of ten years were not to be admitted to the cemetery except under the control of an adult parent. The clerk was instructed to arrange for some bricks to be placed on the chimney of the cemetery cottage, with a quarry over the top, in an attempt to remedy the smoke problem. Thomas Robinson's request for a holiday was granted, provided he arranged for his duties to be carried out in his absence, but most probably not by William Pearson whose claim against the Burial Board was about to be heard in the County Court.

The hearing was held before the Judge, Mr Rupert Kettle, on Tuesday 18th May at Stourbridge. Mr Stokes appeared on behalf of the plaintiff William Pearson, Sexton of Christ Church Lye, and Mr George Perry on behalf of the defendants, The Lye & Wollescote Burial Board.

Mr Stokes stated that Mr Pearson's claim was based on Section 32 of the Burial Boards Act which provided that after the consecration of any burial ground under the Act, the Sexton of the ecclesiastical parish in which the cemetery was situated should perform the duties and functions relating to the consecrated portions of the cemetery, and the interments of the parishioners that took place therein, as he had previously performed them in connection with the parish, and had a right to continue in his office. The Board, however, did not think so and had appointed a man at a working salary to do the duties in place of the plaintiff who now laid claim to all the fees to which he was entitled for all the interments that had taken place in the consecrated portion of the cemetery since the appointment of the other person. There had been twenty-eight such burials in the consecrated portion of the cemetery up to the time of commencing the action and Mr Pearson was, therefore, entitled to £4 18s 0d in fees. Mr Stokes also put in a claim for damages on account of Mr Pearson being deprived of the office of Sexton at the cemetery and applied for an injunction to restrain the Burial Board from engaging any other person to perform the duties.

Mr Perry, on behalf of The Lye & Wollescote Burial Board, objected and stated that Christ Church Lye did not form an ecclesiastical parish within the meaning of the Act, and that the plaintiff had not been legally appointed. He went on to argue that the plaintiff was appointed by a churchwarden to dig the graves at Christ Church and not by the incumbent and could not, therefore, bring an action.

However, the Judge decided that Lye was an ecclesiastical parish within the meaning of the Burial Boards Act and that the plaintiff, at the time of the formation of the Lye & Wollescote Burial Board, was Sexton of such parish and was entitled, therefore, to a verdict for the loss of fees amounting to £4 18s 0d. The Judge also considered that the plaintiff was entitled to the sum of five pounds damages in addition to the fees, and granted the injunction applied for by Mr Stokes.

On learning of the outcome of the case, the Board's solicitors, Messrs Freer & Perry, were instructed to appeal against the Judge's decision but this appears to have been unsuccessful leaving the Board with no choice but to allow William Pearson to dig graves in the consecrated portion of the cemetery and to pay his usual fees of 3s 6d for opening 5 ft graves and 5s 6d for those of 7 ft.

Having two Sextons working in the cemetery would inevitably have led to occasions when Thomas Robinson, the Board's appointed Sexton, would have been digging a grave on one side of the cemetery whilst at the same time William Pearson was digging a grave on the other with the 'imaginary line' dividing the cemetery into two halves keeping the men apart.

The continuing problem with smoky chimneys, it seems, was having an adverse effect on the interior of the cemetery lodge as in July of 1880 Mr and Mrs. Robinson applied to have their house painted and papered. The Chairman reported that he had seen the chimney and that a bricklayer had said that it needed to be taken down and re-built at a height of three feet above its present dimensions. The Board seems to have avoided ever reaching a decision on the re-building of the chimney but, in the meantime, it was agreed to paint and paper the lodge at a cost of five pounds.

The year 1880 has been something of a troublesome one for the Burial Board, so it must have been particularly irksome to learn at their last meeting of the year in December, that the clerk had been served with yet another County Court summons at the suit of William Pearson claiming Sexton's fees in the sum of £1 2s 6d. These fees had actually been paid on the 8th of October, some days before the date of the summons, and the clerk produced a letter dated 23rd November 1880 from Mr Pearson's solicitors stating that no further proceedings would be taken in the matter.

The following year of 1881 passed relatively trouble-free except for the fact that, despite having erected a galvanised pipe and cowl on the chimney of the lodge in June, in December the Robinson's reported that it was still smoking so badly that the doors had to be kept open.

The Board's problems with William Pearson surfaced again in January of 1882 when the clerk, on behalf of the Board, wrote to him asking him to fill up graves dug in the consecrated section of the cemetery, but received no reply to his request   Throughout the rest of the year Mr Pearson's activities continued to cause concern to the Board and in November it was resolved to write to the churchwardens of Christ Church complaining of his inefficiency. The Board were of the opinion that he was incapable of properly performing the duties and requested, if possible, that he be removed from the office as regards digging graves in the cemetery.

It appears that among Mr Pearson's shortcomings was an incident where he had not dug out a large enough grave, causing the coffin lid to be wrenched off, and on another occasion he had opened the wrong grave, in which a body had been deposited and the funeral service read. The deceased's relative had then complained that it was the wrong grave and the body was taken out and placed in the chapel until the right grave was opened and the body re-interred. However, despite the Board's complaint to the churchwardens, no action appears to have been taken by them, but it was apparent now that the Board was quite determined to dispense with William Pearson's services and in March of 1884 the Clerk again wrote to the churchwardens about his conduct.

On the 21st of April a special meeting of the Burial Board was convened to discuss the removal of William Pearson and it was resolved to supply the churchwardens with copies of the charges against him. A deputation was appointed to attend the Vestry meeting to arrange for a compromise with Pearson for the resignation of his office at a sum not exceeding £30, the offer to be made without prejudice.

However, at a meeting of the Board the following month the deputation reported that no arrangement had been made with Pearson and the clerk produced a bill received from him for fees of £25 2s 0d in which he claimed nine shillings for a grave which had actually been dug by Thomas Robinson. In June a committee was formed to negotiate with Pearson for the settlement of his present claim and for the surrender by him of all further claims against the Board.

On the 17th of June 1884 William Pearson appeared before the Board when, after some discussion and consideration, he agreed to accept £24 14s 0d in discharge of his claim for fees plus the sum of thirty pounds as compensation for future claims. The committee recommended also that a sum of £54 14s 0d be paid to him in full satisfaction and discharge of all present and future claims. Thus did the Burial Board finally part company with William Pearson who had been a continual thorn in their side since the opening of the cemetery some five years earlier.

In October of 1884, following the departure of William Pearson, the Board asked Thomas Robinson to name a sum for which he would undertake the whole of the work at the cemetery. However, at the age of seventy-two Mr Robinson obviously did not wish to undertake any extra work and in December he informed the Board of his inability to do this. The Board, whilst expressing its regrets, resolved that the matter remain in abeyance. Thomas Robinson continued as Sexton for several more years, though later he did acquire an assistant to act as his deputy.

William Pearson died in January of 1886, at the age of seventy-four years, and was buried in the consecrated half of the cemetery in a grave, if not dug by Thomas Robinson himself, most probably under his supervision. When William Pearson's wife Mary Ann died two years later, she was not buried with him but in another plot a short distance away. Today their graves have completely disappeared.

On the 21st November 1888 Thomas Robinson wrote a letter to the Board tendering the resignation of himself and his wife. This was accepted, subject to six months' notice, and it was left with the Sexton, if he should get better, to remove [from the lodge] as soon as was convenient. The clerk was instructed to advertise immediately for a new Sexton and Caretaker and, just one week after Mr Robinson had handed in his resignation, a special meeting of the Board was held to elect his successor.

Seventeen applications were considered and eventually the Board elected David Powell, a 44-year old former colliery labourer, as their new Sexton with his wife, Patience, as Caretaker. In selecting David Powell, it seems that the Burial Board had learned from having had to deal in the past with two elderly Sextons, the litigious and problematical William Pearson and the constant grievances of Thomas Robinson.

Thomas Robinson didn't live long enough to serve his six months' notice; a few weeks after tendering his resignation he died at the cemetery lodge on the 3rd of January 1889 at the age of seventy-seven. He was buried in the Nonconformist section of the cemetery as was his wife, Eliza, two years later. At a meeting of the Board in April, it was resolved that the services of the late Sexton should be recognised in the form of a memorial to be placed in the cemetery and that the clerk should solicit subscriptions from present and past members of the Board and from the public to that end.

This plan was thwarted, however, as on the 13th of August a letter was received from Thomas Robinson's widow, Eliza, declining to accept the amount subscribed towards her late husband's headstone. The reason is unknown but perhaps she felt aggrieved at the rather indecent haste with which her husband's successor had been appointed, or maybe it was due to all those years of having had to put up with the smoky chimneys at the cemetery lodge.

David Powell served as Sexton at the cemetery for over twenty years. He and his wife died in the 1920s and both were buried in the cemetery, though no headstone marks the spot. Only the grave of Thomas Robinson, the cemetery's first appointed Sexton, still exists today. (Pictured below).

Chapter 3

THE CONTINUING YEARS

In 1882 the first incidence of vandalism occurred in the cemetery. The clerk (substantiated by the Sexton) informed the Board that on the 5th of February several persons had committed damage in the cemetery and it was resolved to take proceedings against them. Two of those involved were Albert Moore of The Hayes and George Perry of Brook Street. William Moore and Richard Perry, parents of the two lads, appeared before the Board and asked that proceedings not be taken against them. After consideration it was resolved that on their collectively paying ten shillings to the Friends of the Stourbridge Dispensary and the cost of 100 placards to be posted in or near the cemetery giving notice of the charge and stating the terms on which the Board had refrained from prosecuting, no proceedings would be taken.

Over the next few years the Burial Board provided certain amenities for the benefit of those attending funeral services, with the provision of suitable stoves for warming the chapels by hot water for which Mr Attwood submitted the designs, and an estimate was obtained for providing, fixing, painting and varnishing twelve pitch pine bench seats for visitors to the cemetery.

When the land at Docker's Farm had been purchased there were mature trees already in existence on the plot. As work on the creation of the cemetery progressed some of those trees were felled and disposed of to the best advantage. However, it is known that at least one mature tree, a Scots Pine, was retained and in 1880 a circular seat was erected around the tree. This tree was the subject of another incidence of vandalism in 1886 when Joseph Taylor of Talbot Street was caught in the act of cutting off the top.

1930's Postcard

Tree Planting

As in large parks and gardens during the Victorian era, the Scots Pine was a popular species for planting in cemeteries, and many of those planted originally in the cemetery are still in existence today particularly bordering the central pathway leading from the chapels. Other fir trees in the cemetery are obviously of a much later planting.

Yew trees, found growing in churchyards everywhere, are seen as a symbol of everlasting life but have a significant pagan meaning being sacred to Hecate goddess of the underworld and magic. Yew trees, however, have a more practical use in that they were unpalatable to livestock and as such were a common tree for planting in graveyards and cemeteries. There are two quite mature yew trees near to the chapels in the consecrated section which, judging from their size, were most probably planted at the time of the laying out of the cemetery in 1878 and can certainly be seen on a postcard printed in the 1930s. Another species of yew can be found on the other side of the pathway which divides the cemetery.

The monkey-puzzle tree, much loved by the Victorians, can grow up to thirty metres in height which suggests that the specimens in the cemetery today were most likely planted at a later date. The tree's sparse foliage was believed to deprive the devil of a hiding place from where he might observe funerals and steal the souls of the departed.

This combination of evergreen trees with conical shapes and dark foliage, together with the avenue of lime trees leading from the entrance gates to the chapels, created the typical 'garden cemetery' of the mid-nineteenth century; a pleasant last sanctuary for the dead and an uplifting place where relatives and friends could visit the graves of their deceased kin amid scenic surroundings.

27

Monuments and Memorials

The majority of the headstones in the cemetery are very typical of the late nineteenth and early twentieth century depicting angels, crosses of various sizes, upright arched or rounded headstones, marble or granite obelisks, broken columns entwined with ivy and simple ground-level kerbstone graves. With a few exceptions those headstones were created by local stonemasons such as Burgess, Davis, Parsons and Willetts, all of Old Hill, Dallows of Blackheath, C. Brown & Son of Hagley Road, Stourbridge, and Jones of both Stourbridge and Dudley.

By the early twentieth century more than six thousand of the town's citizens had been taken to their final resting place and some prominent and interesting memorials had appeared in the cemetery, some of which are worthy of special mention and all can still be seen today.

One of the most common of funereal monuments is the urn, symbolising mortality, though there is only one of this type in the cemetery. It is to be found on the grave of Demarius Davies, wife of Samuel Paddick Davies, who died on September 6th 1909. The draped urn, which stands on a stone pillar covered with a tasselled cloth, signifies the last partition between life and death. (Pictured below).

There are several graves adorned with angel monuments, representing the angel of God guarding the dead. By far the largest is the angel standing on a stepped plinth holding an open book, which can be found on the grave of Susannah Parish who died in 1902, wife of Thomas Parish of Careless Green House who died in 1916.

There are two ridged casket-style gravestones in the unconsecrated section, one of which is on the grave of Lucy Jackson who died in 1881 and her husband, Benjamin, who died in 1887. The other is a memorial to Mary and Joseph Pardoe. Mary Pardoe's inscription tells us that she died on Christmas Day of 1901 and that her husband, Joseph, who died in 1906, was 'For 60 years Superintendent of the Methodist New Connexion Sunday School'.

A small obelisk, like a miniature Cleopatra's needle, rises from the grave of Henry Millward which bears the unusual inscription: 'Whose earthly life closed October 17th 1896, aged 77'

Possibly the most curious and unusual memorial in the cemetery is that which stands on the grave of Mercy Taylor who, according to the inscription, died on the 4th of September 1904. It was erected as '*A loving token from her daughter, Mary Ann Barns*' and takes the form of a white ceramic heart, symbolising love and devotion, set on a brown ceramic tree trunk about eighteen inches high which has the name 'North Bitchburn Coal Co Ltd, Darlington' stamped on the back. This rather strange memorial has created an, as yet, unsolved mystery. There is no record of the burial of Mercy Taylor in 1904 but there is a record of her burial on the 18th of October in the previous year of 1903!

The monument to Thomas Rhodes is perhaps the most impressive as it is the only one of its kind in the cemetery, and is an appropriate memorial to a man who played such an important part in the industrial development of The Lye (See Chapter 4). It takes the form of an anchor set against rocks surmounted by a cross with a chain linking the two together. The rocks are a symbol of everlasting strength and the anchor represents 'hope' or 'at rest'. Early Christians used the anchor as a symbol of St Clement who, in the first century, was bound to an anchor and dropped into the sea.

The headstone of Leah Taylor is unique to the cemetery, being the grave of a Salvationist and depicting the badge of the Salvation Army (See Chapter 5). The inscription, carved on a stone shield set against rocks, reads 'Leah Taylor for 30 years the devoted wife and true comrade of Staff Captain Job Taylor'.

Several more prominent memorials and headstones appeared in later years; by far the largest of these, a solid-looking, grey granite obelisk (pictured above), can be seen in the centre of the cemetery marking the grave of Joseph Thomas Worton, Justice of the Peace and County Alderman, who died in 1936. It is matched by a seemingly identical memorial in Section A to the Brooks family of fruit and vegetable fame in Lye. Both of these memorials were produced by Dallows of Blackheath.

The cross, usually mounted on three graduated steps signifying 'faith, hope and charity', is a potent symbol of Christian faith and there are crosses of various types in the cemetery. The two largest are on the graves of Philip Round, and his brother, James, (See Chapter 4). The cross on Philip Round's grave is the larger of the two and bears a crown representing heavenly reward; a faithful Christian. The stonemason was Jones of Stourbridge.

Another monument of note is that which marks the grave of Maria Fradgley, who died in 1933, and her husband, George Harry, who died in 1937. This distinctive black marble obelisk with its gold lettering is surmounted by a Greek-style pediment and was created by Dallows of Blackheath.

The monument on the grave of Edward Hill and his family is another striking example of the art deco style. The pediment around the tall square column is adorned with little winged cherubs and atop the column stands a cross (See Chapter 4).

Most of the headstones in the newer sections of the cemetery are of the fairly standard design of the later part of the 20th century, but the stone on the grave of William Ernest Nicholls of 'The Mount' Brettell Lane, who died in October of 1955, is quite outstanding. This towering black headstone is at least seven feet or more in height and Mr Nicholls' name appears on the back of the stone as well as the front. The stonemason who created this giant among gravestones was Jones of Dudley.

Chapter 4

PIONEERS OF INDUSTRY AND POLITICS

Henry Wooldridge, died Feb 18th 1913 aged 73

As far as it is possible to take one individual and say that he or she typifies a town, then Henry Wooldridge must typify The Lye. Of humble birth, with little or no education and no family wealth, he started his own business and made a success of it. In addition he introduced a new trade into the town and was possibly the first and only man in Lye to build houses for his workers.

To say that Henry Wooldridge was born of humble birth is very much an overstatement, for his circumstances were impoverished as were most of the nail makers in Lye at that time. Of all the manual workers none perhaps were more exploited, more oppressed or, indeed, more robbed like the old nail makers and that was the environment into which Henry Wooldridge was born. At the age of eight he was making nails, so whatever education he did have would have been very limited.

Without any help from his parents Henry eventually got together enough capital to start his own nail-making business and, when the nail-making trade was in decline, he turned to making horseshoes. However, when that didn't prove a profitable venture he went into the manufacture of 'frost cogs'. A 'frost cog' was a device shaped like a chisel which screwed into the horseshoes in order to give the horse a sure footing in frost or snow. If a horse, encumbered with the shafts of the cart, fell and broke a leg leaving the creature unfit for work, it could ruin a man's livelihood, so frost cogs were an important part of the transport of that day. There were problems with the early screwed frost cogs in that when they broke, the horseshoe had to be removed and replaced. This was a costly process and meant having to take the horse off the road but along came Henry Wooldridge with the idea of a having a self-fastening frost cog which, after some early opposition, became acceptable amongst people who used horses.

Henry had no formal education other than Sunday school and evening classes. Nevertheless his command of the English language and his knowledge of history were quite astounding. This is clearly illustrated in a paper on horseshoes and frost cogs which he presented to the Royal Scottish Society of Arts in Edinburgh in June of 1886.

Henry was quite a cultured man who, amongst other things, taught himself to play the flute and, when he became more affluent, bought himself a silver flute. He also taught himself to play chess and was an avid collector of chess pieces. When the Free Library and Technical School opened in Stourbridge in 1905 it did so with an exhibition which included his collection, then regarded as being one of the finest in the world - quite remarkable for a man of such humble beginnings.

Henry Wooldridge was associated with many of the organisations in Lye, notably the Workers' Institute. He was a great traveller and during his lifetime visited America, Canada and almost every country in Europe. An interesting and rewarding life was that of Henry Wooldridge.

John Ebenezer Hill, died 24th May 1933, aged 78

Anyone familiar with Gilbert & Sullivan will recall that in the operetta *Ruddigore* they sing of 'ghosts, ghouls, bats, owls and things that go bump in the night'.   This is what came into Denys Brooks' mind whenever he walked between the tombstone of John Ebenezer Hill and that of Henry Wooldridge, as they are directly opposite each other in the cemetery.   One could well imagine them at the witching hour of midnight – Henry sitting on his tombstone and John Ebenezer on his – swapping yarns.   They would have had much to talk about as their lives ran very much parallel. For a while they were near neighbours, Henry Wooldridge living in Bromley Street, before moving to Hagley Road, Stourbridge, whilst John Ebenezer Hill lived at The Hayes.

John Ebenezer, along with his brothers George and Thomas, were among the pioneers of the galvanised hollowware trade.   At one time Lye was the 'home of hollowware' and goods from the town's hollowware factories found their way into the markets of all the civilised countries of the world.   During his lifetime John Ebenezer had two or three factories, one of which was at the bottom of Lower High Street, Stourbridge; later he had a factory at Cradley Heath and one opposite Old Hill Railway Station.   He served on many local bodies; at one time he was Chairman of the old Lye Urban District Council and served also as a churchwarden at Christ Church Lye for a number of years.   In his younger days he was regarded as a very fine athlete, being an accomplished sprinter.   In later years, however, he took up bowling, a game of which he was very fond.

Thomas Rhodes, died May 23rd 1906, aged 78

On the 1881 census Thomas Rhodes is described simply as a 'Bucket Maker' but this modest description belies his true role in the history of Lye. Thomas Rhodes was a pioneer who brought the vitreous enamelled trade into the town. It was always a matter of friendly dispute between Thomas Rhodes and George Hill, another Lye hollowware manufacturer, as to which one of them was first in bringing these trades into the district. A native of Lye, Thomas Rhodes started in business as a maker of alkali drums for use in Lancashire. In 1856 he founded the Providential Works which, when he retired in 1886, passed to his son Robert. The works covered seven acres and by 1894 employed over 150 people. Among the many items produced at the works were baths, bowls, basins, beer and milk cans and, of course, buckets.

Thomas Rhodes was essentially a businessman, and took no prominent part in public life but devoted his spare time to the Wesleyan Methodist Church in Lye where he was a trustee. In fact there are several Wesleyan Churches in the surrounding district where he held this position – at Clent for instance where the church was converted into a private house. A memorial stone bearing his name was in the Wesleyan Church in High Street, Kinver, now demolished, and he was a trustee at the Wesleyan Church at Gig Mill, Stourbridge, also no longer in existence. Thomas Rhodes was a trustee at the New Road Methodist Church in Stourbridge and his name can be seen on one of the foundation stones of the little Wesleyan Church at Gospel Ash, near Bobbington.

Rhodes Buildings in Lye High Street, carries two plaques bearing the inscriptions 'Diligent in Business' and 'Be not Slothful'. These words perhaps sum up the essence of Thomas Rhodes who served his church well and provided work for the people of Lye. Many of the people featured in this book have Thomas Rhodes to thank for their start in life.

Edward Hill, died 27th January 1950 aged 89

Edward Hill was another founder of the hollowware industry, having launched out as a galvanised hollowware manufacturer in the 1890s and carried on successfully until 1909, when his company also incorporated enamelled ware. In 1919 he founded the firm of Edward Hill & Sons of which he was managing director.

Apart from his business Edward Hill was very interested in horticulture and was president of Lye & Wollescote Allotments Association, an office he held up to the time of his death. He never entered public life, his only hobbies being his home and his garden but he was a staunch supporter of Toc H. Around 1945 he made a gift to the Lye Branch of 'Toc Hill Hall' including the land and the building with all its equipment. This is remembered by some as being a rather rickety wooden hut which stood on the corner of Cemetery Road and the main Stourbridge Road. He was very interested in the Darby and Joan movement and, just over a week before his death, had provided and been present at its 'First Birthday' tea. Edward Hill was living in Pedmore when he died, his funeral service being held at St. Peter's Church, with the Reverend H C Burrough, Vicar of Stambermill, officiating at the interment in Lye Cemetery.

Frederick Eveson, died 6th November 1922 aged 49

The Eveson family has been known in Lye since the mid-nineteenth century: first in the nail-making trade and, when that was in decline, for a short time in chain-making but eventually they went into the hollowware trade. Frederick Eveson was one of two of the original founders of the firm of Eveson Bros, hollowware manufacturers.

Frederick Eveson, son of Elias Alexander and Ann Maria (Perry) Eveson, was twelve years old in 1885 when his eldest brother, George Harry (whose story is told in Chapter 8), lost his life in tragic circumstances. Many years later the respect and esteem for Fred Eveson of Eveson Bros was manifested at his impressive funeral at which his father, Elias, was one of the mourners. Along the route to the cemetery blinds were drawn and at the gates and in the cemetery itself an immense crowd of people gathered representing trades and businesses from throughout the district and a wider area. The funeral cortege consisted of ten mourning coaches containing sixty people. Members of several Masonic Lodges were present, who filed by the grave and dropped their tokens of remembrance on the coffin, a fitting tribute indeed to Frederick Eveson.

Philip Round, died 12ᵗʰ January 1936 aged 76

Another well-known name associated with Lye's
hollowware trade was that of Round. Philip Round,
proprietor of the works of Messrs J & P Round of
Orchard Lane, received his early education at Lye
Church School but was working by the age of ten.
With keen initiative and careful attention to detail
he rose to become one of the foremost hollowware
manufacturers in the district, a trade in which he
had had a good grounding having worked as a boy
for both Thomas Rhodes and George Hill, those two
pioneers of the hollowware industry.

Philip Round's father was in the nail-making
business and his grandfather was an anvil and
vice-maker. Philip assisted his father for a while
but in 1875 he started in the hollowware trade and
worked with his brother James until 1924 when
James retired. Philip Round continued by himself
and in 1929 took over the works of Thomas Hill.
The Round factory workshop, established in 1849
as a nail-making business in Orchard Lane (now
Lye By-pass), is still in existence - a rare reminder
of the days when industry in Lye was flourishing.
It is understood that the workshop has been 'locally
listed' by Dudley Council and is among buildings in
the borough considered 'worthy of protection and
conservation'.

Philip Round lived at one time
at Brocksopp's Hall and later,
when he had Iverley House built
at Norton, the staircase was moved
from Brocksopp's to his new
home. Although of a somewhat
retiring nature Philip Round was a
benefactor to numerous charities.
He had a life-long connection with
St John's Methodist Church, Lye
and for thirty years was a Chapel
trustee. In 1921 Philip and James
Round paid off the debt on the
Chapel and Philip had electric light
installed in the Church in memory
of his father.

James Round died a few years before Philip and the brothers are buried side by side in Lye Cemetery.
On James's grave is recorded the death of his only son who gave his life in the Great War of 1914-
1918 at the age of 20.

Joseph Richard Hurdiss, died 11th April 1939 aged 71

The nail making trade, the frost cog industry and the hollowware industry have all been mentioned, but over and above all these was the brick making industry. It was said that Lye Cross was the centre of one of the richest seams of fire clay to be found anywhere in England and, as a consequence, quite a number of brickworks existed in Lye. Many of these brickmakers lived in Lye but then, as they grew in wealth and status in the community, moved out to more salubrious areas like Hagley or Pedmore. Joseph Richard Hurdiss, however, remained true to Lye and lived and died in the town.

Joseph was the proprietor of the Hadcroft Brickworks in Shepherds Brook, known as the Lye 'red and blue brick company'. Of all the brickyards in Lye only two ever put the name 'Lye' on their bricks and Hadcrofts was one of them. This particular brickyard was set up to make the blue bricks for the Stourbridge viaduct built to replace the original wooden structure designed by Isambard Kingdom Brunel.

A story has been handed down that the blue brick building to the right of the entrance to Old Swinford Hospital in Heath Lane was built with bricks made for the Stourbridge viaduct and which had 'fallen off the back of a cart'.

Stourbridge Viaduct, built in 1882

Entrance to Oldswinford Hospital

Alice Perks, died 28th June 1928, aged 69

Alice Perks must rank as a pioneer with regard to women's involvement in the political scene in Lye. Forget everything you have ever read or were ever taught about Mrs Pankhurst and the suffragette movement because, in the opinion of Denys Brooks, the history books had got it all wrong.

In 1896, seven years before Mrs Pankhurst started the suffragette movement, twenty-two years before women had a vote (and then only a partial one), and twenty-three years before Mary Astor became the first woman Member of Parliament, Alice Perks went along to a meeting of Lye Parish Council and had the audacity to propose the names of twelve women to be members of that Council. This surely must have been the first instance of 'women's liberation'. So it could be said that both 'women's suffrage' and 'women's lib' began in Lye.

Amos Perrins, died 29th June 1928, aged 60

Amos Perrins who died, coincidentally, the day after Alice Perks, was an ardent supporter of another lady involved with local politics. The lady in question was Mary Macarthur, founder of the National Federation of Women Workers and leader of the Women Chainmakers Strike in 1910.

Amos, father of the well-known Lye historian, Wesley Perrins, left school at a very early age and started work as a boy at Corngreaves Iron Works. He then went into the brick-making industry where he took a prominent part in a strike when over one thousand workers came out from Lye, Cradley Heath, Brettell Lane and Brierley Hill. This made Amos very unpopular and, for a while, he couldn't get any work but eventually went into the business of making frost cogs.

Amos Perrins was a member of Lye Urban District Council for many years and when he became a Justice of the Peace was one of the first working men to be so appointed. He always took a keen interest in politics and if anyone feels they would like to thank somebody (or possibly blame somebody) for the fact that this country had a woman Prime Minister then Amos Perrins is probably the man. It was he who took a prominent part in the nomination of Mary Macarthur to be the Labour candidate for Stourbridge in the 1918 General Election. This was the first time that women (those over the age of 30) were allowed to vote, and Mary Macarthur was one of seventeen women candidates who stood for parliament in 1918. She lost to the Liberal candidate, the Right Honourable J.W. Wilson by 1,333 votes.

It could be said that Lye, not to mention Amos Perrins, helped blaze the trail in support of women in parliament, paving the way many years later for the election of the country's first woman Prime Minister.

Frederick Kitson, died 18ᵗʰ May 1892, aged 40

It is perhaps unusual to find such an elaborate headstone for a man who was a humble horse nail maker in Lye but Frederick Kitson, who died at the comparatively early age of forty, was the forefather of a family that founded one of the most important steel companies in the Black Country. His son, another Frederick Kitson born in 1876, worked at the Birmingham Trading factory in Dudley Road where he started his working life by gathering bundles of steel and eventually rose to become manager of the factory.

Around 1916, at the age of forty, Frederick Kitson purchased the factory from his boss and in 1927 founded the Lye Trading Company in Pedmore Road. Over the next forty or more years Frederick Kitson, succeeded by his sons and grandsons, built up what can only be described as an empire with an annual turnover that ran into millions. By the 1970s the company was delivering around 190,000 metric tonnes of steel products per year throughout the United Kingdom and had warehouses not only in Stourbridge but in Wales, Scotland, Middlesex and Yorkshire. In 1974 the company was acquired by the British Steel Corporation but the old Lye Trading Company is still identified with the Kitson family, whose rise to success from such humble beginnings is an example perhaps of how 'great oaks from little acorns grow'.

Frederick Kitson died in 1967 at the age of ninety and the factory in Dudley Road (now Portway Tool & Gauge) is said to be haunted by his ghost who stands on the stairs watching the workers coming in. Sadly, the ornate headstone in Lye Cemetery commemorating his parents Frederick and Emily, photographed intact some years ago, today lies in pieces; like many in the cemetery, the target of vandalism in more recent years.

Chapter 5

PREACHERS AND RELIGIOUS LEADERS

Charles Thomas Dickens, died 17th November 1929, aged 63.

It is arguable if there is another burial ground in England where you could expect to find the graves of five men, and five working men at that, who together formed their own religious society in 1891 and built their own chapel – the Bethel Chapel in Hill Street – which is still going strong today. Charles Thomas Dickens was one of those five men and it was in his home that the first services of the Bethel Chapel were held. He was a very able speaker but did his most useful work in the Sunday school. Unlike his famous literary namesake, this Charles Dickens was a blacksmith who, in his early days, worked for Thomas Rhodes.

It is interesting to note that in July of 1993, Charles Dickens' great-grandson was ordained a curate in the Church of England. Whether or not Charles would have approved of that is impossible to say but an old Lye centenarian, Mr Harry Hill – a life-long member of the Bethel Chapel - was known to have commented that Charles Dickens' great-grandson had 'gone over to the enemy' typifying the rift that once existed between church and chapel in Lye.

Alfred Wooldridge, died March 8th 1931, aged 82

Alfred Wooldridge, another of the five who established the Bethel Chapel, was a marvellous preacher. Again, a man with very little education but a poet of no mean order with some of his poems being used as hymns at services at the Bethel. When he died, the minister who conducted the service, instead of delivering a eulogy, read some of Alfred Wooldridge's own poems.

Amos Perrins

Amos Perrins, featured in Chapter 4, was another founder of the Bethel Chapel.

Albert Newton Perks, died January 2nd 1941, aged 73

Very little is known about Albert Newton Perks, another founder, other than the fact that he served as secretary to the Bethel Chapel for over forty years and surely this is testimony enough for where would any organisation be without its secretary. One definition of how a secretary works was given in a sermon by a Salvation Army officer who likened the secretary of any organisation to a 'swan gliding seemingly effortlessly across the water whilst underneath the surface the legs were going like the clappers'.

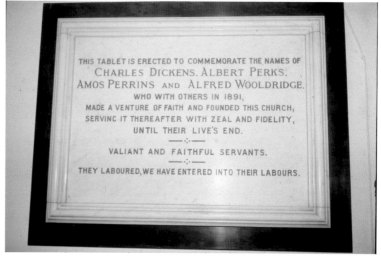

Five working men were named as founders of the Bethel Chapel but the commemorative plaque on the wall inside the chapel names only four: Dickens, Perrins, Perks and Wooldridge. The fifth man was Henry Homer and although he was, indeed, one of the founders of the chapel, through some misunderstanding before the chapel really got going, he transferred his allegiance to the Salem Chapel in Pedmore Road, where he became a trustee.

Reuben Kendrick, died 21st August 1948, aged 85

Reuben Kendrick started work in the hollowware trade which, as previously stated, was quite a lucrative industry both for the masters and the men. He was a local preacher at the Salem Chapel but felt the call to higher things, sold up his home and entered the Church Army, a uniformed organization of the Church of England, founded in 1882 by the Reverend Wilson Carlisle with whom Reuben Kendrick was a pioneer in the early days. However, he did not stay long with the Church Army but joined the Missions for Seamen, which in itself was quite remarkable when you consider how far Lye is from the sea. Reuben Kendrick served the Mission for 40 years and at his funeral his coffin was draped with the 'Flying Angel' - the banner of the Missions for Seamen. His wife Eliza Hannah (known as 'Lizzie'), a faithful mission worker with her husband, was one of the Lees family who were local farmers in Wollescote and Pedmore.

Alfred Morris, died March 17th 1956, aged 88

In 1782 William Hutton, the Birmingham historian and bookseller, published his book *A History of Birmingham* in which he wrote words to the effect that if anyone would like to see what ancient Briton had looked like they would see it on the road from Stourbridge to Birmingham at a little place called Lye, or 'Mud City' as he described it - and Lye has had what might be termed 'a bad press' ever since. So it is hoped that the following four inhabitants of Lye cemetery, all of whom produced sons who went into full-time Christian work in one church or another, will in some way serve to redeem the heathen impression created by William Hutton.

First and foremost is Alfred Morris, a well-to-do Lye businessman in the watchmaker and jewellery trade, and a prominent member of St Mark's Church, Stambermill. Two of his children died at an early age but he saw one of his sons, Alfred Edwin Morris, attend the Church of England School, after which he joined his father's business in Stourbridge Road, Lye. Alfred then went into the army and afterwards decided to enter the teaching profession, becoming Professor of Hebrew at Lampeter College. Later in his life he was appointed Bishop of Monmouth, eventually becoming Archbishop of Wales, the only non-Welshman to be so appointed. Alfred Edwin Morris was one of Lye's more honoured sons.

Thomas F. Rhodes, died May 12th 1943, aged 76

Not to be confused with the aforementioned Thomas Rhodes of bucket-making fame, this Thomas F. Rhodes was the father of John Clarence Rhodes, ordained a Deacon in 1929. After serving in Wednesbury for a time, John Clarence Rhodes served the greater part of his ministry in the Potteries. For some time he was also a clergyman at Berkley's Hospital in Foregate Street, Worcester.

Percival Thomas Hancock, died 10th March 1971, aged 79

Percival Hancock was an ordinary working man and, in fact, had one of the dirtiest jobs it was possible to do in the hollowware trade. He was what was known as a pickler, a job which entailed immersing the hollowware products into a bath of acid in order to remove the dirt and rust Percival Hancock's son, Leonard, progressed to Stourbridge Grammar School and eventually became a clergyman in the Church of England and in the early 1990s was serving at All Saints in Loughborough.

George Albert Aston, died 22nd April 1950, aged 83

George Albert Aston had two sons: one was Claud Aston, an erstwhile Mayor of Stourbridge, the other was Vernon Gladstone Aston whose early education was at Scott's School in Stourbridge and later at the Grammar School. He became a clergyman and spent most of his ministry at Penkull in the Potteries. He was quite a talented man who wrote and produced pantomimes for the parish and was also the author of a little book of poems.

Hannah Pearson, died April 28th 1930, aged 83

A mention should be made of Hannah Pearson's son, Albert, who left Orchard Lane School at the age of twelve and went to work for a Cradley Heath engineering company. When old enough he became a local preacher and a Methodist minister in 1911. Some years ago Albert wrote a letter to the 'Black Country Bugle' in which he told of the day he had to attend the examination for his acceptance as a candidate for the ministry. He found himself standing at the Five Ways in Cradley Heath, an appropriate spot as Albert had reached a turning point in his life. After debating with himself as to whether he should turn right and go to Graingers Lane Church for his examination, or whether he should turn left and go back to Holt & Willets where he had worked for a number of years, he decided to turn right and was accepted as a minister. When he died in Cornwall, at the age of 102, Albert Pearson was the oldest minister in the Methodist Church.

Leah Taylor, died 27th September 1915 aged 51

One of the most interesting graves to be found in Lye Cemetery is that of a Salvationist – Mrs Staff-Captain Leah Taylor. The date of birth of the deceased is not often shown on a gravestone but one of the kerbstones at the side of Leah Taylor's grave states that she was born in Lye on 4th August 1865. What is a little out of the ordinary is the fact that the other kerbstone bears the words 'Promoted to Glory 1915'. Not 'departed this life' or 'passed away', as is usual on a gravestone, but 'Promoted to Glory'. However, the front kerbstone is a real gem, for it bears the words 'Saved by Grace 1880' which refers to Leah Taylor's conversion.

It seems that at about the age of fifteen, whilst on a visit to Kidderminster, Leah saw half a dozen Salvation Army lasses kneeling down in the street and this so impressed her that she took her stand as a Salvationist. This was in 1880 and, as the Lye Corps of the Salvation Army was not founded until 1881, it clearly suggests that Leah was a founder member.

Leah Taylor had four children, two sons and two daughters and, like most Salvationists, her children also followed that religion. Her two sons married two sisters, the daughters of General Higgins who became Commander-in-Chief of the Salvation Army on the death of Bramwell Booth, son of the founder General William Booth. One of Leah's sons was, for a time, editor of the 'War Cry' and, just prior to his death, had been appointed as Commissioner for the whole of the western seaboard of America. After his death his widow married General Albert Osborn. Most of Leah's family, at one time or another, served on the Salvation Army's International Staff and Leah's husband, Staff Captain Job Taylor, was on the personal staff of General William Booth.

The last two lines on Leah Taylor's headstone are, 'Reader, think! Are you right with God', so it could be said that even from the grave Leah Taylor is still preaching the Gospel.

Chapter 6

PERSONALITIES OF LYE

Robert Thomas Webster, died 6th November 1922 aged 64

Robert Thomas Webster was possibly one of the most colourful characters ever to have lived in Lye. He ran an antique business on Lye Cross, known as 'Ye Olde Antique Shoppe', and seems never to have passed up any opportunity to advertise his trade. In 1896 his wife died and, about two years later, Mr Webster declared his intention to lay kerbstones around the grave bearing the inscription: **'S.A.J. Webster wife of R.T. Webster of 'Ye Olde Antique Shoppe Lye'.** The marble stones were ordered from a stone mason in Old Hill who then applied for permission to put them in place but the local Council refused on the grounds that the inscription carried an advertisement and advertisements of private businesses could not be allowed in the cemetery. Not to be outdone, Webster waited his chance and, on an occasion when the Sexton was working elsewhere in the cemetery,

recruited some friends to help him put the stones in place. When the Council got wind of this they held a meeting actually in the cemetery. The news spread like wildfire and soon a crowd of several hundred people had gathered and three constables were brought in to keep order. As a consequence of the meeting, the stones were removed and placed outside the cemetery gates which were closed and locked at five o'clock. Mr Webster, ever resourceful, then took the stones back to his shop and displayed them in his shop window. In that respect the Council had played into his hands because he had more publicity than if the stones had been in the cemetery.

Sooner or later, he decided to have another go at putting the stones around his wife's grave and on a certain day when he knew the Council would be absent from the district, he and nine other men armed with trowels, sand, cement and iron staples again put the stones around the grave. At this point the Council decided to hold a public meeting in an attempt to clear up the matter but while they were deliberating a piece of the kerbing was broken away and removed. This led to Webster offering a reward of fifteen pounds to anyone giving information about the stolen portion of marble kerb.

The 'Webster' Chair

Around 300 people attended the meeting which became disorderly and broke up after half an hour. Sometime later R T Webster was elected to the Council and the affair gradually died down. It was almost certainly these events which gained him the nickname 'Wily Webster'.

In 1900, four years after the death of his wife, Webster was again causing tongues to wag in Lye with the announcement in the newspaper that ...*considerable interest had* been *evinced in the marriage of Mr R.T. Webster of 'Ye Olde Antique Shoppe...'* It appears that he had acquired a second wife. On the 7th November at St Matthews Church, Malvern Link, Robert Thomas Webster, at the age of fifty years, married Miss Catherine Preston, aged thirty-nine, daughter of the late Mr John Preston of Footherley Farm, near Lichfield which had been in the family for 200 years. A year or so later Webster's new wife presented him with a daughter.

Robert Webster was not a native of Lye but was born at Mere Pool, Sutton Coldfield where he worked as an assistant in his father's blacksmith and farrier's business. At the age of twenty, and with a yearning to travel, he decided to set sail for Australia. Due to the unpunctuality of the trains, however, he arrived at the port of Liverpool only to find that the ship had sailed without him. He then responded to an advertisement for a blacksmith in Lye and came to work for Mr John Abel so Australia's loss was Lye's gain. After working for Mr Abel for a while he set up in business for himself near Lye Cross as a hay and straw dealer. After almost losing his life when one of his hayricks caught fire he became a broker and established the business for which he was to be best known and most successful, that of antique dealer.

Mr Webster established himself also in public life. He was a member of the Board of Guardians for many years and became a member of The Lye Urban District Council in 1899, donating an ornately carved chair for the use of the chairman. Among his many other interests he was a staunch supporter of the Cottage Homes Scheme, a member of the Hearts of Oak, being a delegate for the Stourbridge District, and founded the Society's Old Boys' Association. He donated a silver challenge cup for the annual cricket match and other silver cups to the works' clubs of Lye and the United Clubs Bowling League.

R T Webster was immortalised in a novel called *A Bitter Debt: A Tale of the Black Country*, published as a serial in *The People's Friend* - a Scottish periodical. The story was penned by the romantic novelist 'Annie S. Swan' (Mrs Burnet-Smith) who for a short time lived in Lye in the early 1890s when her husband Dr J Burnet-Smith was an assistant to Dr Thompson of Cradley, having charge of the old surgery at Hay Green. Mrs Burnet Smith made the acquaintance of Mr Webster, whom she described as 'quite a philosopher in his way', when purchasing curios and antiques from his shop. She later introduced him as a character in her story and, in fact, quite a number of characters in the book could be identified as people she had met during her sojourn in Lye.

On Monday the 6th November 1922, a few days after celebrating his 22nd wedding anniversary, Mr Webster went to preside at a meeting at Stambermill Congregational Chapel in support of the Right Honourable J W Wilson, M.P. who was seeking re-election for the Liberal party. Shortly before the commencement of the meeting Mr Webster was seen to be taken ill. He was carried into the vestry and both Dr Darby and Dr Hardwicke were summoned but, sadly, Mr Webster had breathed his last. Dr Hardwicke certified that the cause of death was heart failure and no inquest was necessary. The funeral took place on Friday the 10th of November and R T Webster was buried in Lye Cemetery.

There is, however, an unusual twist to this story. At the spot in the cemetery where Webster, his first wife and also his second wife, Catherine, who died in 1936, were supposedly buried there is no grave, no headstone, no kerbstones just an empty plot of grassy ground. It seems ironic that, having gone to so much trouble to mark the spot where his first wife lay, there is now nothing to mark the last resting place of R T Webster of 'Ye Olde Antique Shoppe in Lye'.

William Hugh Riley Pearson, died 18th June 1923 aged 48

In the early days of education Lye Council used the school rooms of the Congregational Church, a commodious building with a large assembly hall. Orchard Lane School which replaced it never had the luxury of a school hall. William Hugh Riley Pearson, a member of a well-known Lye family, was among the first intake when Orchard Lane School opened in December 1882 and, at a very early age, became a pupil-teacher at the school. Today much is written about school inspections but they are nothing new and existed in the early days of the Education Act. Then an inspector would not only inspect the fabric of the school, but also the staff, the scholars and the board of governors and, if he found anything amiss, it would be entered in the school log book for all to see. The log book of Orchard Lane School, now kept at Worcester County Record Office, has such an inspector's report which carries the rather blunt entry, 'W H R Pearson – Failure'. How heartbreaking it must have been for a fourteen-year old lad to have the word 'Failure' written alongside his name. This particular lad, however, was made of stern stuff. He persevered with his studies and later took a two year course at Carmarthen College where he qualified as a teacher.

Later on in life he decided to study the law and was eventually called to the Bar in June of 1907. It is doubtful if there are any barristers, at least in England, who were called to the Bar in more glamorous circumstances than was William Hugh Riley Pearson. For one of those also called to the Bar that night happened to be a royal prince - Prince Arthur of Connaught - grandson of Queen Victoria and nephew of King Edward VII. Among the many distinguished guests were two Indian Maharajas, a Vice-Admiral, two Lieutenant-Colonels, six Knights of the Realm and Mr Rudyard Kipling. Not bad company for a lad who started life in Cross Walks, Lye and was deemed a failure at the age of fourteen by the inspector of Orchard Lane School.

As a post-script to this story, in 1912 when Stourbridge Urban District Council successfully presented their petition for borough status, leading counsel for the petitioners was William Hugh Riley Pearson. A promising career was ended by his premature death at the age of forty-eight.

William Knowles, died 8th April 1893 aged 62

The remarkable story of William Knowles is quite relevant to the present day when a 'job for life' has become largely a thing of the past. Gone are the days when a young man could leave school, enter a trade and know that if he kept his nose clean he could most probably stay in that trade for the rest of his working life. There are many today who, with the ever-soaring cost of living, have to resort to holding down more than one job to make ends meet. In the mid-nineteenth century William Knowles was just such a person.

On the 1861 census, his trade was given as that of nail maker, as were many others of the Knowles family in Lye at one time. However, being an intelligent man, William realised that sooner or later the nail trade would cease and ten years later, on the 1871 census, his trade was shown as shopkeeper for he was then running a co-operative shop in Dudley Road, Lye. It seems that in the 1860s two co-operative stores were opened in Lye, the first of their kind in the whole of the Birmingham area. By 1881, however, William Knowles was working at yet another trade, that of carpenter and painter.

When he died in 1893 the notice of his death in the newspaper described him as a carpenter, painter and coffin maker. This death notice gave a brief summary of his life and revealed he had other strings to his bow: he was a well known and well respected Primitive Methodist local preacher, a member of the Liberal party and had been a key worker for the Temperance movement, being one of the original trustees of Lye Temperance Hall. Such was the respect he commanded that it seems 'all Lye turned out' to see William Knowles buried, the whole occasion being quite a moving experience.

The inscriptions on William Knowles's gravestone are a testament to his life. Just below the headstone is the statement that the stone was 'Erected by Public Subscription'. On the left hand kerbstone are the words, 'For 36 years an earnest temperance worker', on the right hand kerbstone it states 'For 34 years a faithful local preacher', and at the foot of the grave are the words 'I'm Blessedly Saved'.

Mary Ann 'Polly' Brooks, died 11th January 1931 aged 72

Lye has produced two Knights of the Realm. One was Sir Cedric Hardwicke and the other was Sir Michael Higgs who represented Bromsgrove in Parliament for a number of years. However, Lye also had a 'Lady' in her own acclaim if we are to believe the headline of her obituary which read, *'Lye Loses Lady Bountiful'*. The 'Lady' referred to was Mary Ann Brooks, known throughout Lye as 'Polly Brooks', eldest daughter of Joseph Brooks who founded a fruit, vegetable and poultry business in the town.

When her father died Polly Brooks took over the family business and, on the death of her brother, Thomas Henry, also took on the licence of the 'Old Cross' public house. After the death of her brother, Jeremiah, in September of 1922 Polly took complete control of the greengrocery business with branches in Cradley Heath and Kidderminster and farms at Hodge Hill, Kidderminster, Woodfield, Ombersley and Whittington. She had a reputation of being an astute business woman not only in the local market but around the world - in the markets of America, Canada, Jamaica, Brazil, Holland and Belgium. Anywhere, in fact, where fruit and vegetables came from Polly Brooks was known. As a single individual she was probably the largest purchaser of bananas in England!

She was very wealthy and, for the poorer people of Lye, her death was a tragedy for of those who went to Polly for help, few were refused. Denys Brooks – no connection as far as is known to Polly's family - had his own anecdote relating to her generosity. He came from a working class family and believed this particular incident must have occurred at a time when his father was out of work and there was not much money coming into the house. One Sunday morning Denys's mother had skinned

a rabbit for the family's Sunday dinner but found it had been badly bruised by the trap. She went straight up to Polly's shop to complain and old Polly took one look at the rabbit and ordered one of her servants to replace it with a duck. That, Denys said, was the only time in his life he could ever recall having duck for Sunday dinner.

Robert Brettell MBE, died 16th October 1951 aged 66

Robert Brettell spent 32 years in the coal mining industry and was awarded an MBE in the New Year's Honours List of 1948 for his services to that industry. He died less than a month after his retirement as manager of the Beech Tree Colliery which, before it became part of the National Coal Board, had belonged to Messrs Mobberley & Perry Ltd. Robert Brettell had also been manager of three other Mobberley & Perry pits at Oldnall, The Hayes and The Dingle. Formerly he had held the position of manager at the Spon Lane Colliery, West Bromwich. In 1924 he was President of the National Association of Colliery Managers encompassing South Staffordshire, Warwickshire and Worcestershire. A Freemason, he was a member of the Regis Lodge, Old Hill for several years.

Robert Brettell was a man with diverse interests and excelled in all his various pursuits. He was a well known philatelist and exhibited in Paris and New York where in 1936 he won a bronze medal. He also received awards from the Birmingham Philatelic Society in 1935-1936 and 1937-38. He was keenly interested in music and was a vocalist and a banjo player of high repute. In his younger days he did a great deal of concert work and organized concerts for charity during the First World War. He was an enthusiastic gardener and specialised in growing roses and chrysanthemums gaining several prizes with the latter. He was fond of cycle racing and, again in his younger days, took part in many amateur races. He enjoyed cricket and attended the county games regularly. Until about ten years before his death he was a member of the Churchill & Blakedown Golf Club and won the 'Fenn' challenge cup in 1935-36, a competition open to members of the Colliery Managers Association. And if all that wasn't enough, he also took a keen interest in the history of the locality. All in all, Robert Brettell was a successful and accomplished individual who seems never to have wasted a single moment of his sixty-six years.

Charles Thomas Dickens, died 20th January 1963 aged 75

Lye can boast of having not one Charles Dickens buried in it's cemetery but two - the second Charles Dickens being a nephew of the one featured in Chapter 5. This Charles Thomas Dickens was also a blacksmith by trade and worked for more than fifty years for Messrs. Chas. Dickens & Sons of Attwood Street, Lye. However, the musical notes on his headstone are something of a giveaway as to his life-long passion. At the age of twelve years he began as an organist at the Bethel Chapel, Lye where his namesake was one of the founders. In his early years he was connected with Stourbridge Choral Society and for over fifty years was organist and choirmaster at St. John's Methodist Chapel where he trained the children for more than fifty consecutive Sunday School Anniversaries. His gravestone also bears the name of his wife, Obedience, who died ten years after her husband at the age of eighty four. It is a name virtually unheard of in today's modern world but would not have been at all out of place in the nineteenth century novels of Mr. Charles Dickens.

Pharoah Adams, died 26th January 1924, aged 54

The name 'Pharoah' is unlikely to feature in any 'top ten' of boys' first names today; indeed it was an unusual name to encounter even in the nineteenth century, but it was an extraordinary name for an extraordinary man. Pharoah was a larger than life character and one of Lye's best known and most popular inhabitants, and no name was more familiar in the home or in the street than that of 'Pharoah Adams' which is how he was most generally called, as very few people ever used the prefix 'Mister'.

Pharoah Adams was a self-made man who began life in Rowley Regis, the son of a shoemaker. Pharoah himself was making shoes at the age of eleven but he soon left that trade behind and went to work in the boiler yard at Danks's of Netherton. When only about sixteen or seventeen years of age he launched out into the butchering business and had the satisfaction of seeing this venture prosper to the extent that eventually he opened shops at Old Hill, Halesowen, Netherton, Brierley Hill, Stourbridge and at Lye which became his home and headquarters. Success attended him in every direction and he became a familiar figure in the cattle markets of all the Midland counties including Gloucestershire, Oxfordshire and Cheshire. Over the years he rented farms at Hunnington, where he resided for a time, at Careless Green and, in later life, Sugar Loaf Farm at Norton near Stourbridge where he founded the Galloway races in 1922.

Pharoah Adams was a sporting man with a penchant for trotting ponies and owned one of the best trotters in the world, a pony of just over twelve hands called 'Jimmy', on whose behalf an open challenge was issued on three successive years. Pharoah won some notable races with this pony at Liverpool, Blackpool, Manchester and Stockport. At the time of Pharoah's death his pony, 'Jimmy', was twenty-four years old, having been pensioned off some ten years earlier to live a 'life of lazy grandeur'. One of Pharoah's last wishes was to see his beloved pony.

To say that Pharoah Adams was a generous man is something of an understatement. It was no uncommon thing for him to walk down Lye High Street emptying his pockets of a considerable sum to people he met who sought his assistance. However, it was his great generosity during the First World War and the coal strike of the 1920s for which he was best remembered. Almost daily he provided meat or money to one or other of the many funds and causes at that time. He gave liberally to the soup kitchens and provided meat sandwiches at the Temperance Hall for all the schoolchildren of The Lye & Wollescote, for which he roasted no fewer than ten hind quarters of beef. At Netherton he gave the old people a meat meal and provided a concert in the Public Hall after which he gave each woman half a pound of tea and each man two ounces of tobacco. At Lye

54

he donated a handsome gold watch to be auctioned, the proceeds going to a fund raised on behalf of Lye & Wollescote soldiers and sailors who had lost limbs in the war. During the war when meat was short, Pharoah Adams was able to tap into sources that no other butcher could reach and used his own motor car to travel vast distances to see that food reached the district.

One story that has passed down the family, and which perhaps typifies the eccentricity of the man, is that every Thursday he went to the meat market in Birmingham and on his return he and a companion, after partaking of considerable alcoholic refreshment, would race their ponies and traps from the top of Mucklow Hill to the 'Gypsies Tent' hostelry on a wager for a pint. As both men urged their horses along the road, local folk would come out of their homes to see this exciting spectacle and, more often than not, Pharoah would be ahead at the end of the race. Pharoah Adams was, indeed, one of Lye's great personalities, whose his name is well-remembered today throughout the district.

Reta Mary Bellamy, died 25th September 1994, aged 100

When Denys Brooks first presented his talk on Lye Cemetery in September of 1993 this headstone was one of his curiosities. At that time Reta Mary Bellamy's name was inscribed on the headstone despite the fact that she was still very much alive and about to celebrate her 100th birthday in October of that year. Reta Mary Bellamy dedicated her life to the service of the community and was known as a kind, approachable lady. During the war she did sterling work for the National Savings movement and in 1963 she was presented with a gift to mark forty years of voluntary service at the Child Welfare Clinic in Orchard Lane. Reta lived in Valley Road and was a regular worshipper at Christ Church Lye. In September of 1993 she was living in a residential home in Tamworth and, as her 100th birthday approached, she made a special request to take part in a service at Christ Church to mark the grand occasion. Leaders at the Church organised a special communion service to be held at 5 o'clock on the Sunday of her birthday followed by refreshments and Reta returned home to Lye to celebrate her centenary.

Almost a year later in September of 1994, Reta Mary Bellamy returned home once again to Lye but this time it was to be buried in the cemetery beneath a stone which already bore her name. When she died the name 'Bellamy', possibly one of the oldest names in Lye, died with her.

Chapter 7

PHYSICIANS AND PUBLIC FIGURES

Dr Henry Darby, died 22 January 1937 aged 68

Henry Christopher Darby was a doctor in Lye for forty-five years. Not only was he concerned with the health of the body, he also cared for the well-being of the soul. For many years he was connected with the Congregational Church where he did much useful work. On Sunday nights Dr Darby would hold a magic lantern lecture for the children and was involved in the organization of a particular movement where the children of his class formed into a group calling themselves the 'Golden Opportunity' messengers. The aim of this group was never to miss an opportunity of doing a good deed, an endeavour which perhaps some of today's children would do well to emulate.

Apart from his work as a doctor, Dr Darby was involved with the Lye Branch of the St John's Ambulance Brigade which was the equal of any in the country. One story told about him was that on one occasion he was on his way to Redditch and came upon a scene where a man had suffered a haemorrhage. Dr Darby was able to save the man's life and, after that event, he donated the 'Christopher' challenge shield, a trophy competed for every two years amongst ambulance and nursing divisions in Worcester for the arrest of haemorrhage.

Although reputed to be amongst the first people in Lye to own a motor car, in his earlier days Dr Darby travelled around by pony and trap. It appears that the source of supply of ponies to pull the traps was the local hunt. After a horse had passed its 'sell-by date' as far as working in the field was concerned, the animal was still quite useful for a number of years to pull a little trap for some business or professional man. People who keep pets – cats, dogs and the like - will know that they all have their own little idiosyncrasies and it would seem that horses are similarly affected. Dr Darby's horse, during his hunting days, had a habit of dropping his ears onto the back of his head before taking a jump. The story goes that one day Dr Darby was trotting along the road from Lye to Stourbridge in his pony and trap. As they approached the old wooden viaduct at Stambermill, the horse dropped his ears back as if preparing to jump over the obstacle, at which the good doctor is said to have cried out, 'Under this one, you fool!'.

Dr Edwin Hardwicke, died 26th August 1932 aged 72.

Another well-known Lye doctor was Edwin Webster Hardwicke. He and his wife, Jessie, were members of St Mark's Church, Stambermill and Mrs Hardwicke especially did a great deal of work for the church. Her name can often be found in old newspaper reports of events at St Mark's – providing refreshments, managing a stall or helping to arrange a concert. Then suddenly, and without explanation, their involvement with the Church ceased. Religion is regarded by many as a bulwark against the 'slings and arrows of outrageous fortune' but sometimes, if faced with a personal disaster, faith can crumble. Possibly something of that nature occurred in the Hardwicke family when their daughter, Muriel Burne Hardwicke, died in 1904 at the age of seven years. In his time Dr Hardwicke saved many lives in Lye but was powerless to save the life of his own child. When he died in 1932 Dr Hardwicke's family requested that 'no obituary notice should appear in the newspapers, and that his funeral should be of the simplest nature, and should interfere as little as possible with the normal life of the community in which he worked, and which he loved.'

Dr Hardwicke was, of course, the father of Sir Cedric Hardwicke, once described as one of the finest actors of his day. In his youth Cedric Hardwicke was involved also in the affairs of Stambermill Church. In fact, on his seventh birthday he made his theatrical debut at a concert held in Stambermill day school which was organized to raise funds for Sunday school prizes. It was said that his mother did much to encourage young Cedric's interest in theatrical work, and that was true to a certain extent. However, there was another lady who had more to do with Cedric's early life than even his mother and that lady was Alice Taylor, nee Allen.

Alice Allen was a nanny with the Hardwicke family and, when Cedric was a lad, it was she who provided all his first props and make-up. Along with his mother, Alice encouraged his theatrical ambitions and Cedric Hardwicke never forgot her; whenever he was appearing in London he would always send her a couple of tickets. In 1935, when he opened the Branch Library in Lye, he admitted quite openly that it was no use his coming to Lye and playing the role of a 'big man' for, as he said, 'There is someone in the crowd who used to bath me when I was a child', referring, of course, to Alice Allen. Sir Cedric talked quite a lot about Alice (Allen) Taylor in his autobiography, *A Victorian in Orbit*, relating the story that when Alice got married and went on her honeymoon she didn't take her husband with her.

Nevertheless, Alice and her husband Frederick were married for over fifty years. They died within two days of each other in 1954, both at the age of eighty-three, and were buried together in Lye Cemetery.

Owen Freeman, died 5th October 1908 aged 64

It is said that on the memorial to Sir Christopher Wren in St Paul's Cathedral can be found the words, '*If you would see a monument to his works, look around you*', words which should perhaps have been inscribed on Owen Freeman's gravestone.

Owen Freeman was born in Belbroughton, Worcestershire and for many years his family were in the building trade. In his early years Owen himself worked in that particular trade in partnership with his brother but around 1870 he moved into Lye and commenced working as manager of the large brickworks of George King Harrison. He was a man very much involved in public service being a member of the Burial Board, a member of the School Board, a churchwarden at Christ Church, Lye and an architect of no mean order. It was Owen Freeman who designed the steeple that once stood atop Lye Church and was responsible for the design of the Salem Chapel in Pedmore Road, where every one of the 30,000 bricks used in the building were donated by one or other of the local brickworks including 10,000 white bricks from George King Harrison. Owen Freeman also prepared the designs for the Bethel Chapel which opened in 1900, and other structures which can almost certainly be attributed to him are Rhodes Buildings in High Street and the redbrick and terracotta Centre Buildings on the corner of Lye Cross. So, like Christopher Wren in London, monuments to the works of Owen Freeman can be seen in The Lye & Wollescote to this present day.

Joseph Darby Cartwright, died 17th August 1930 aged 72

Road traffic accidents, often resulting in fatalities, are now almost a daily occurrence but in the 1930s, when there was far less traffic on the roads, they were not so commonplace. So when one of Lye's most prominent and well-known citizens was knocked down and killed by a motor car the news caused a sensation in Lye and the surrounding district. Joseph Darby Cartwright, who lived at 'The Hill' in Lye, had attended Corbett Hospital Fete on August Bank Holiday Monday and the following day, Tuesday the 5th, he left for a holiday in Blackpool. On the night of Friday the 15th of August at about ten o'clock Mr Cartwright was returning to his hotel with a friend, Mr Morris of Worcester, when only yards from the hotel both men were struck by a car. Mr Morris was badly injured but Joseph Cartwright failed to regain consciousness and died from his injuries the following Sunday the 17th of August His tragic death caused profound shock in his home-town of Lye as, despite being almost seventy-three years of age, he had been in the best of health and appeared to have many years of public service ahead of him.

Born in Mears Coppice, near the boundary of Lye and Quarry Bank, Joseph Cartwright was cradled in Methodism, his father having been a well-known local preacher in his day. Mr Cartwright and his wife worshipped at Mount Tabor Chapel where they were frequent benefactors. Immediately after his school days, he worked for a few years at the Corngreaves Iron Works and then went into the goods shed at the Great Western Railway Station, Lye rising to the position of foreman. However, being of a progressive nature, Mr Cartwright (much against the rules of the Company) opened a boot and

shoe business in premises situate in the High Street opposite Valley Road, later occupied by Adams Brothers butchers. Soon after attaining the position of foreman at the goods shed he resigned and took an appointment with Flowers, the brewers of Stratford-on-Avon. Eventually he became the representative of Edward Rutland, wine and spirit merchant of Stourbridge. After a period of this work he accepted an appointment as a traveller for Messrs Chaters, boot manufacturers of Kettering, and for about thirty years covered a very wide area of the Midlands and the Eastern counties for that company. At the outbreak of the Great War, the firm of Chaters was taken over by the Government and Mr Cartwright gave up travelling, installed a manager in his Lye shop and retired to live at 'The Hill', which he had purchased from Mr Rhodes, where he spent much of his day-time leisure in gardening.

Just before the First World War, Mr Cartwright entered into public life in Lye, at one time being one of the three members of the Stourbridge Board of Guardians. He was a keen educationalist and for many years was a member of the Lye School Managers and served as its Chairman for five consecutive years. He was also a member of the Stourbridge Higher Education Committee and the Stourbridge District Elementary Education Committee. In his later years he took up bowling and was one of the founders of the Lye Private Bowling Club. He spent most of his summer evenings on the green and was presented by the members with a beautiful alabaster clock which stood on the mantel piece of the drawing room at 'The Hill' bearing an inscription with the date 1904. For twenty-five years he was a 'sleeping partner' in the firm of Rhodes & Cartwright, hollowware manufacturers of Cradley Heath, of which his brother, Fred Cartwright, was the chief and acting principal. On July the 27th 1879, Joseph Darby Cartwright married Alice Maud Mary Griffin of Mount Pleasant, Quarry Bank and they celebrated their Golden Wedding anniversary in 1929. It was almost a year later to the day that Joseph Darby Cartwright was killed in a road traffic accident whilst on holiday in Blackpool.

Rufus Dunn, died 18th September 1965 aged 82

Rufus Dunn of Crabbe Street, Wollescote was another well-known public figure. He first entered public life in 1918 when he was co-opted as a member of the Lye and Wollescote Urban District Council in place of William Chance who retired through ill health. In the election after the First World War, Rufus Dunn was returned to the Council as a Labour representative and became its vice-chairman. At the end of his term of office he did not seek re-election until the triennial elections in May of 1931 when he was again elected as a Labour member. In the following year he became the last chairman of Lye Council before the district was amalgamated with the Borough of Stourbridge.

He became a member of the Stourbridge Council and in 1945 was chosen as Mayor of Stourbridge, being only the second Labour member to hold such office. During his term as Mayor he observed strict impartiality and as a result of his refusal to participate in Labour Group affairs he was not re-elected for a second term as Mayor.

Rufus Dunn had a varied and impressive record of involvement in public service. For eight years he was a representative of the Council on the Board of Governors of King Edward VI School, Stourbridge and for over ten years he was Chairman of Crabbe Street School managers. He became a Justice of the Peace for Worcestershire in 1931 and in 1934 he was elected chairman of Stourbridge Main Drainage Board. In 1952 he was chosen as vice-chairman of the Stourbridge Bench, a position he occupied for several years.

For many years he was very prominent in the trade union movement in the West Midlands after serving a full apprenticeship in the local firebrick trade. For thirty-nine years he was a member of the National Union of General and Municipal Workers, being secretary and treasurer of the Stourbridge No. 1 Branch and for twenty years he was a district organizer in the Birmingham and West Midlands Area of that union, retiring in 1947. At various times he served as vice-chairman of the National Joint Wages Board for the refractory industry, was operatives' secretary on the Stourbridge Firebrick Wages Board, a member of the National Joint Council for the building brick industry, operatives' secretary on the Regional Council for the salt-glazed ware industry and served on the Hollowware Workers' Council. He served on the Executive council of the NUGMU and represented that union at the Trade Union Congress. He also served as chairman of the East Midlands Cast Stone Joint Industrial Council, vice-chairman of the Needle & Fishing Tackle Joint Industrial Council and was workers' representative on the non-trading Joint Industrial Council for the West Midlands.

Rufus Dunn was brought up in the Band of Hope movement and from 1900 to 1930 he was secretary of the Lye Temperance Society. In 1919 he was district president of the Sons of Temperance Friendly Society, served as treasurer of Lye Temperance Hall and was a trustee of the hall for many years. In 1929 he succeeded Amos Perrins as president of the Lye & Wollescote Labour Party.

After his retirement he devoted much of his time to the Road Safety Movement and for many years was chairman of the Stourbridge Road Safety Committee. He represented Herefordshire, Warwickshire and Worcestershire on the National Road Safety Executive Committee and served as a member of the Council of the Royal Society for the Prevention of Accidents.

Rufus Dunn had a long association with the Lye Ebenezer Methodist Church where he and his wife Harriet had married in 1909, celebrating their Golden Wedding in 1959. They lived in Wollescote all their lives and had five sons. Mrs Dunn died a year before her husband in October 1964.

Chapter 8

HISTORY IN THE HEADSTONES

Titus Webb, died 16ᵗʰ May 1881 aged 85

The gravestone of Titus Webb is unique to the cemetery in that it records the fact that he was 'For 46 years a citizen of the United States of America'. His story gives us an insight into the experience of thousands of migrants who, like Titus, sailed across the Atlantic in the first half of the nineteenth century in search of a new and better life. Within fifteen years of the opening of the Erie Canal in 1825, New York had become the busiest port in America and, as settlers poured west, immigrants from Europe and Britain arrived in the city where, if you were enterprising enough, there was money to be made.

Titus Webb was born in Kingswinford in 1796, the youngest child of Benjamin Webb and his wife Phoebe. The Webb family were scythesmiths and spade makers, with the exception of Titus who left these shores to seek his fortune in America, a perilous undertaking to say the least. In the days of sailing ships it took around six weeks to cross the Atlantic but adverse winds or rough seas could make the journey twice as long. Titus, along with the majority of passengers, would have travelled in the cramped conditions of steerage with no privacy whatsoever and, prior to 1842, passengers had to provide and cook their own food. The biggest dangers the immigrants faced was that the ship would catch fire or they would be shipwrecked. In those early years many ships left the shores of England and failed to make landfall.

Exactly when Titus Webb set sail on his great adventure is unknown but it seems likely that it was sometime in the early 1830s as he is recorded as living in Mott Street, New York in 1835. He would have witnessed the great fire which devastated the entire business district of New York in December of that same year. Regarded as American's first great disaster, at its height the fire was visible for a distance of a hundred miles. Titus would have seen the city re-built with wider streets and finer buildings and, within seven years of the fire, become an even greater city than it had been previously and the financial capital of the world. Charles Dickens, visiting New York in 1842, described it as a 'beautiful metropolis...with fine streets of spacious houses and green leafy squares'. Titus Webb must have enjoyed living there as, in 1847, he applied to the Marine Court of New York for naturalization, thus becoming a fully fledged American citizen.

Sometime before 1840 Titus had married Catherine, though nothing is known about her other than the fact that she was born in Scotland. The couple do not appear to have had children and Catherine remains a shadowy figure in the background. By 1852 Titus was firmly established as a Crockery Ware Merchant in New York City but by 1860 he and Catherine had moved out to the township of Morrisania (now incorporated as a neighbourhood in the Bronx) where they lived on the west side of Washington Avenue with Titus owning real estate to the value of $10,000. Titus appears to have made several trips back and forth across the Atlantic, his last trip being in 1860 when he sailed from England on the S.S. 'Vigo', arriving back in New York on the 7th of November, a few months before America was plunged into its most bitter conflict – the Civil War.

Titus Webb, then in his mid-sixties, took no active part in the war but the effects were felt in his home-town of Morrisania.   At the outbreak of the war Oliver Tilden, a resident of the township, enlisted in the Union Army rising to the rank of captain. He was killed in combat in Virginia in September of 1862 and was Morrisania's first casualty of the Civil War. His body was returned to his hometown to lie in the Memorial Hall on the corner of Washington Avenue. Captain Oliver Tilden is remembered today in the name of a small park called Captain Oliver Triangle, located in the Bronx neighbourhood.

Sometime after 1870 Catherine Webb died and Titus returned to England where in 1881, aged 85 years and a widower, he was living in High Street, Lye with the Hyrons family. John Hyrons was a boot manufacturer, a local Methodist Preacher and a member of The Lye & Wollescote Burial Board. His business in High Street was next door to Lavender's Gents Outfitters. John Hyrons' wife, Susannah, was Titus Webb's great-niece and another great-niece, Eliza Webb, was in the Hyrons household acting as his nurse. Titus died of old age on the 16th of May 1881 and was buried in the cemetery where his gravestone records the fact that he had lived more than half of his life in America.

George Harry Eveson and Albert William Brooks, died 6th July 1885, aged 17

In the summer of 1885 the town of Lye suffered the loss of two of its young men in a tragic drowning accident. George Harry Eveson, son of Elias Eveson a chain maker, and Albert William Brooks, son of William Brooks a grocer, were both born at the end of 1867. They had been close friends throughout their lives and worked together at the galvanising works of Messrs Thomas Rhodes & Sons, bucket manufacturers of The Lye.

On Monday the 6th of July 1885 a large party of workpeople from the works went to spend their annual holiday at Upper Arley on the River Severn, among them George Eveson and Albert Brooks. These two young men, in company with another young man named Griffiths, went down the river a little way to bathe and, unknowingly, selected a most dangerous spot near the Victoria Bridge. At the side of the river the water was quite shallow but a little way out there was a sudden dip of some twenty feet or more. At first George and Albert stayed in the shallow water whilst Griffiths, the only swimmer of the three, struck out to see whether the water was safe for his companions. However, before he could warn them that he could not find his depth, they had followed him and immediately were struggling helplessly in twenty or thirty feet of water. Albert was said to have risen but once and then disappeared, and George Eveson tried to save himself but was also drowned. The river was dragged for some time and subsequently both bodies were found and conveyed to the 'Harbour Inn' to await the inquest where subsequently a verdict of 'Accidental Death' was returned.

The funerals of George and Albert took place on Friday the 10th July at half past four in the afternoon. Long before that time the townspeople of Lye had gathered along the approaches to the cemetery, and the pathway into the cemetery was so crowded that it was difficult to see how the

procession would reach the chapel. Some one hundred and twenty nine men, boys and girls employed at Messrs T Rhodes followed the coffins and each of the girls carried a wreath of flowers or a floral tribute in the shape of a cross. Reverend A Wright of St Mark's Church, Stambermill read the service in the chapel and at the graveside where the two friends were laid side by side with only a foot or two of earth separating them. Mr Thomas Rhodes himself gave out the hymn: *'Thy will be done'* and afterwards the workpeople who had followed the two young men to the grave lined up on either side of the pathway leading to the entrance gates and remained in that position till all the family mourners and friends had departed. Today only the gravestone of George Harry Eveson survives in Lye Cemetery to tell the tragic story of the drowning at Arley on that summer's day in 1885.

Sarah Knowles, died 24th August 1888, aged 61

The inscription on the headstone of Sarah Knowles tells its own story.   It reads:
In loving memory of Sarah
wife of Joseph Knowles who fell asleep in Jesus on the
platform of the Railway Station at Shrewsbury'.

On Friday the 24th August, Sarah Knowles was returning with her daughter, Priscilla, from an extended visit to the town of Shrewsbury. They had driven to the railway station in an omnibus with the intention of catching the 1.25 p.m. train back to Lye. As they got out of the omnibus Mrs Knowles became agitated thinking they would miss the train, as it was already in the station, and she walked rather hurriedly across the bridge over the line. At the first carriage she put her foot on the step to get in but was informed by a lady already inside the carriage that there was no room and she was keeping the places for someone else. Mrs Knowles said, 'There's room for two ma'am. I'm feeling ill, let me come in'. There was no porter around at the time and Priscilla Knowles took her mother's arm and led her away to try to find a seat in another carriage. They passed along two or three but couldn't find a seat and Mrs. Knowles said to her daughter, 'Take me somewhere to sit down. I shall die this time'. She at last sat down on a truck on the platform and Priscilla could see that her mother was dying. Someone connected with the railway went to fetch some water but Sarah Knowles died immediately.

At the inquest it was revealed that she had had a similar attack some time previously and was under medical attention from Dr Thompson of Cradley who stated that 'the deceased's heart was weak and he had felt that if she had another turn, as before, she would most probably succumb to it'. In her excitement to catch the train, Sarah Knowles did indeed succumb and breathed her last on the platform of Shrewsbury Railway Station, a fact recorded on her headstone.

Benjamin Wakeman, died 20th January 1897, aged 82

Benjamin Wakeman, and his father before him, occupied a stall in the old Stourbridge market where they were known as the 'oatmeal men'. Oatmeal in those days was evidently a much-used commodity and not only did the Wakemans sell oatmeal, they also milled it. Benjamin Wakeman had his own little mill at Stambermill where he ground the oats, but it appears that the Drainage Board altered the course of the stream and he was forced to abandon his mill.

It could be argued that this particular stream was the one which powered the mill mentioned in the Domesday Book. In the survey for Old Swinford only one artefact is mentioned - a mill - which it is believed gave its name to Stambermill. Today the name 'Stambermill' is spelt as one word. On Benjamin Wakeman's gravestone it is shown as 'Stamber Mill', but originally it was made up of three words: 'stam' being Saxon for stone, 'ber', a corruption of 'burn' or 'stream' and 'mill' which is obvious. It could be said that Benjamin Wakeman's headstone takes Lye's history right back to the Domesday Book.

At the foot of the gravestone can be seen the name Elizabeth Wooldridge, a daughter of Benjamin Wakeman and wife of Henry Wooldridge featured in Chapter 4.

Meshach Lavender, died 25th February 1890 aged 66

Meshach Lavender was a master tailor; he and his descendants were tailoring in Lye for a hundred years or more yet probably during all that time they never made more than three dozen suits for the men of the town. The story of Meshach Lavender is like the story of Lye itself – full of oddities. Whilst the working men of Lye would most likely have been wearing old corduroy trousers, belt and braces, collarless shirts and cloth caps, Meshach Lavender in his shop was making hunting pinks, hacking jackets and jodhpurs for the gentry. Local people could recall a time when Lye High Street was lined with chauffeur driven vehicles, all waiting for their masters who were being measured or fitted for their hunting attire.

However, Meshach Lavender's inclusion in this chapter is not because of his tailor's business but because of the fact that it was in his shop doorway during the elections of 1874 that, it could be said, Lye became civilized. Unlike today when elections are held on one specific day, in those days an election would be spread over three or four days. Dudley would have its election on one day, Stourbridge on another, Droitwich on another and so on. There was a method in that madness insofar as, at that time, quite a few towns experienced rioting when an election was taking place and by spreading the election over three or four days the police force could move around to quell any likely disturbances. On that particular day in 1874 there were, in fact, sixty policemen stationed in Lye.

There was one Polling Station at Lye Cross and, with plenty of free beer around to influence the voters, towards the afternoon things got rather out of hand. So much so that a magistrate from Stourbridge was brought in to read the Riot Act. This is quite a lengthy Act but the actual proclamation, read on occasions like this, was just one terse sentence. The consequence of reading this proclamation by the magistrate was that the police or militia could charge the unruly crowd and if anyone was injured, maimed or even killed then nobody could be blamed. It was in Meshach Lavender's shop doorway that the magistrate from Stourbridge chose to read the Riot Act, but the crowd failed to disperse and the police were forced to charge. The ringleaders were apprehended and brought to Worcester Assizes where they appeared before the Lord Chief Justice of all England and sentenced to three months hard labour.

It appears that this was the last occasion that The Lye nail makers made what was known as a 'Tiss-as-Twassis' or 'Tis-as-it-was'. This was a fiendish device of a four-pronged sharpened nail which, when thrown on the ground, would always land with a point upwards. Any horses of the mounted militia or police who stepped on these nails would shy and throw the rider but the occasion of the election of 1874 was the last time when the 'Tiss-as-Twassis' was used.

John Abel, died 24ᵗʰ June 1914 aged 78

John Abel had an interesting link with the past. He was born in a house in Dudley Road that Denys Brooks once described as 'one of the stately homes of England', namely the house known as Brocksopp's Hall, where his father before him had had a blacksmith's business until building the forge at Stourbridge Road which John Abel carried on for fifty years. Originally Brocksopp's was a four-storey house reputedly older than Wollescote Hall and when the top storey was removed a priest's hiding hole was discovered. While the Abel family were still living at the Hall one of the workmen in their employ extracted a cannon ball out of one of the beams – a relic of the English Civil War.

In 1675 a man named William Buffery died in the house. He appears to have been a very wealthy man, so much so that he issued his own halfpenny coin which can be found listed in any good handbook on coins and tokens. He was reputed to be the same man who owned the furnaces bearing the name Buffery at Dudley and also gave his name to Dudley's Buffery Park and Buffery Road. Four men were named as 'appraisers' in the last Will and Testament of William Buffery. Heading the list of those appraisers was Nicholas Addenbrooke, one of the first Governors, Feoffees or Trustees – call them what you will – appointed by Thomas Foley, founder of Old Swinford Hospital. The Addenbrookes were a well-known milling family in Lye and Stambermill and lived in the area for many years. A great-great-grandfather of the afore-mentioned Nicholas Addenbrooke was Thomas Addenbrooke, a founding Governor of Stourbridge Grammar School, and a grandson of Nicholas Addenbrooke's brother, Roger Addenbrooke of Kingswinford, endowed and founded what is arguably one of the best known hospitals in the country – Addenbrookes in Cambridge.

Lieutenant Evelyn Victor Turner, died 18ᵗʰ November 1916, aged 36

The First World War took its toll of the young men of the Lye & Wollescote as evidenced by the names on the memorial window in Christ Church. One name that does not appear on the window is that of Lieutenant Evelyn Victor Turner who is commemorated on the cross in the cemetery which marks the spot where his parents and brother are buried.

The Turner family were not originally a Lye family. Joseph Turner, an accountant, was born in Stratford-on-Avon and his wife, Sarah Elizabeth, was born in Welshpool, Montgomeryshire. They married in 1871 and lived for a time in Tipton where a son and two daughters were born. Their youngest son, Evelyn Victor, was born in 1880 when the family were living in Pearson Street, Brierley Hill. Later the family moved to Cemetery Road, Lye, next door to the Reverend Arthur G Lewis, then Vicar of Stambermill. Joseph Turner died in February of 1901 and was buried in the cemetery. Evelyn Victor, aged twenty-one, was at that time employed as a clerk in a Fire Brick Manufactory. At the start of the Great War he enlisted as a private in the Warwickshire Regiment but by 1916 was attached to the 8ᵗʰ Battalion of the North Staffordshire Regiment and had attained the rank of lieutenant.

The Battle of the Somme began in July 1916 and continued until November of that year during which time thousands of men lost their lives.   Sarah Elizabeth Turner and those of her family remaining at home had now moved from Lye to live at 'Stourhurst' in Lower High Street, Stourbridge. While her youngest son was fighting in France, it was there on the 16th of October that Sarah Turner died of heart failure and was buried in the Lye & Wollescote Cemetery with the Reverend Arthur Lewis officiating at her funeral.   Just over a month later, while still grieving the loss of their mother, Lieutenant Turner's brother and sister received the news that he was missing in action.   It was later confirmed that he had been killed during an attack on Grandcourt on the 18th of November, regarded officially as the date on which the Somme offensive ended.

The Thiepval Memorial in France bears the names of more than 72,000 officers and men of the United Kingdom and South African forces who died in the Somme sector and have no known grave. Over 90% of those commemorated died between July and November of 1916.   Lieutenant Evelyn Victor Turner's name is recorded on the Thiepval Memorial and was added also to the cross on his parents' grave in Lye cemetery with the inscription: *'Be thou faithful unto death and I will give thee a crown of life'*.

Ronald Bingham 1914 -1975

This simple headstone has quite a story behind it. The Binghams were an old Lye family and this particular branch lived in Pedmore Road in what, from an historical point of view, could be described as one of the most important houses in the whole of the Stourbridge area. In the Bingham's time it had become a pair of three storey semis but originally had been one house dating from the seventeenth and quite possibly the sixteenth century.

There is in existence an old map of Old Swinford Manor dating back to 1699 on which are marked several front elevation drawings of the more important buildings in the area. One of them is the afore-mentioned Old Swinford Hospital, another Old Swinford Church and Rectory; others named are Wollescote Hall and Wollescote House, Foxcote House, Wollaston Hall and the house where the Bingham's lived, officially known as Lye House but nicknamed 'Porridge Hall', the home of the Witton family for many generations. In the late 1600s the house was the marital home of Francis Witton, a scythesmith, and his bride, Sarah Sarjeant, two of the earliest dissenters in the Stourbridge area. Sarah Serjeant was the daughter of Richard Serjeant of Kidderminster, an evicted minister under the 1662 Act of Uniformity, which required the Prayer Book to be used in all churches. Some two thousand ministers refused to comply with the Act and were ejected from their parishes – one of those ministers being Richard Serjeant, who settled in Hagley.

The Wittons, originally Congregationalists, held religious services in Lye House prior to the opening of the (Independent) Congregational Chapel in Stourbridge in 1689. A hundred years later they had transferred their allegiance to the Unitarian Church and, in the late eighteenth century, another Francis Witton helped found the Unitarian Chapel in Stourbridge. Prior to the opening of the Unitarian Chapel in Lye in 1806, the first place of worship to be built in Lye, religious services were once again held in Lye House, the home of the Wittons.

Joseph Chamberlain MP (1836-1914) was descended from the early Wittons of Lye on his grandmother's side of the family, and the Birmingham hymn writer Thomas Hornblower Gill (1819-1906) was also a kinsman of the Witton family. All in all, the house where the Binghams lived had some quite important historic connections.

Edwin Walter Dukes, aged 25, died 18th March 1929 and Joseph Chance, aged 66, died 18th March 1929.

There is perhaps not a burial ground in the whole of the Black Country, or indeed anywhere in the country where coal was mined, where you would not find a similar gravestone to that of Walter Dukes. Through his headstone, and that of Joseph Chance, is told the tragic story of the Golden Orchard Colliery mining disaster at Coombs Wood, considered to be one of the most appalling tragedies to have happened in the South Staffordshire coalfield during the first half of the twentieth century. Eight miners lost their lives – two of them being Lye men: Edwin Walter Dukes, aged 25, who lived in Bromley Street, Lye with his wife and four-year old daughter, and Joseph Chance, aged 66, of Brook Street who was married with two grown up children and was on the point of retiring.

The Golden Orchard Colliery, belonging to Messrs N Hingley & Sons of Old Hill, was regarded as one of the safest pits in the country and many were left wondering how so simple an accident could have resulted in such a terrible loss of life. The men had descended the pit at 7.30 a.m. on the day shift and were proceeding along the roadway when they discovered that fifty yards behind them the brattice sheet, a tarred canvas sheet fixed for air regulating, had caught fire and they were cut off by the flames. How the fire started was unknown but it was possible that one of the candles carried by the men had come into contact with the sheet as they passed along the roadway. The timber to which the brattice sheet was fixed also became ignited and the men were trapped. At that stage they were not overly concerned as they felt that workers in other parts would get to the fire and 'dout it' but one of the men, 66-year old Jabez Edwards of Old Hill, was not satisfied with this and, after several unsuccessful attempts, eventually managed to make his escape from the blazing main road of the pit. He thought the others would follow him and later said that he left them all 'talking jolly together' believing they would have a better chance by waiting.

Some time elapsed before the fire was discovered by other miners proceeding along the roadway to their work places. The alarm was raised and rescue operations commenced immediately. Attempts were made to extinguish the fire with water and two pumps were taken down the shaft, but the rescuers faced extraordinary difficulties owing to the distance of the fire from the pit shaft. The mine was 800 feet deep and the fire was 300 yards from the pit bottom.

The colliery rescue party were reinforced by the Dudley Rescue Brigade who reached the pit around ten o'clock, having been hampered by the dense fog which prevailed that day. It was not until the Halesowen Fire Brigade arrived at mid-day that any real progress was made. The entombed men had their usual supply of food and drink and it was hoped that they might get a sufficient supply of air to keep them alive. It was 4.30 in the afternoon when the rescuers reached the men who were found fifty yards from the where the fire had been raging. It was evident that all of them had been suffocated by smoke fumes or from carbon monoxide gases as there was no sign of any injury on any of the men.

The bodies of Walter Dukes and Joseph Chance, who were related by marriage, were found quite close together. Walter Dukes was sitting down and had a partially smoked cigarette in his cap. Medical evidence later confirmed that the men had died of carbon monoxide poisoning and all would have been dead by about 9 a.m. The inquest returned a verdict of 'Accidental Death'.

The funerals of the two Lye men were held on the same day. Large crowds lined the route as the two funeral processions left their respective homes and eventually converged on their way to the cemetery. Two or three thousand people had assembled at the gates and along the path leading to the cemetery chapels, with hundreds more taking up positions on the south side of the cemetery near to the graves. Connected as they were by family ties, not only had the two men lived fairly close to each other, they had worked and died together and were buried within a few feet of each other: Walter Dukes in the grave that already held his baby son who had died at the age of four months old some two years earlier.

Joseph Dainty, died 20th June 1941, aged 54

The story of Joseph Dainty is as tragic as any that can be found in the cemetery. Born in Stambermill, his early days were spent working in the brickyards, as did his father and older brother. Shortly after the death of his mother in 1903 Joseph, at the age of seventeen, took the King's shilling and served three years with the Worcestershire Regiment leaving the army as a reserve in July of 1907. It was whilst on furlough in April of that year that he met and began walking out with Anabella Davies, a waitress at the Stourbridge Junction Railway refreshment rooms. They became sweethearts and began making plans for the future.

Anabella's home life, however, was anything but happy. Her parents, particularly her mother, were heavy drinkers and Anabella suffered much mental and sometimes physical abuse as a result of the constant quarrelling between them. Her mother didn't approve of Anabella's association with Joseph Dainty, she claimed that he was jealous of her daughter's friendship with a sailor and had threatened to kill Anabella. On one occasion her mother had accosted Joseph in the street, striking him and calling him names. Anabella frequently spoke of 'ending it all' and Joseph went along with this in order to appease his sweetheart, but he was planning to go to Wales with a friend and when settled intended to send for her and they would be married.

On the night of 29th September 1908, Joseph met Anabella after work and found her in a particularly distressed state of mind, having come home to find that her mother had pawned her clothes. They walked along the canal from Stourbridge and then on towards the bridge at Wordsley. They stopped near the 13th lock about 180 yards from Wordsley Bridge and Anabella told Joseph of her great unhappiness. Suddenly and without any warning she cried 'Goodbye Joe' and threw herself into the water. Joseph jumped in to try to save her but she had disappeared and sometime later Joseph was found on the canal bridge covered with blood having attempted to cut his throat. Anabella's body was later recovered from the canal and taken to the nearby 'Vine Inn'. Later a post mortem examination on her body was carried out by Dr Gifford of Brierley Hill. Joseph was taken to the Infirmary at the Stourbridge Union Workhouse at Wordsley and placed under the care of Dr Arnold Thomson, Medical Officer at the Infirmary.

Two days after the tragedy an inquest was held at the 'Vine Inn' but was adjourned to wait either for Joseph Dainty's condition to improve or, as was fully expected, his death when both inquests could be held at the same time. The funeral of Anabella Davies was held on Sunday the 4th of October and it was estimated that 10,000 people crowded into Stourbridge cemetery on that Sunday afternoon for her burial. Today there is no headstone to mark where she was laid to rest.

Over the next few weeks Joseph Dainty's life hung in the balance but he was sufficiently recovered to attend the adjourned inquest held on the 2nd of December at the Union Workhouse. However, after hearing all the evidence, the jury's verdict was that the couple had entered into a suicide pact and Joseph, as the survivor, was regarded as being an accessory before the fact. He was charged with 'Wilful Murder' and, following a hearing before the magistrates at Brierley Hill, was sent for trial at Stafford Assizes. The trial took place in March of 1909 when the evidence given by various witnesses revealed the true character of Anabella's mother and highlighted the sorry state of affairs in the Davies household which had led to Anabella's suicide. Joseph Dainty was subsequently acquitted of the charge of murder and left the Court room a free man.

Joseph went back to his original occupation of brick maker and four years later at St Mark's Church, Stambermill, married Mary Elizabeth Roper who bore him two sons. There is, however, no happy ending to this story as in 1927, after a long and painful illness, Mary died at the age of thirty-six and was buried in the cemetery at Lye.

Fourteen years later, in 1941, Joseph Dainty was living in a house in Dixon's Green Road, Dudley where he was employed to care for an elderly gentleman. Shortly after nine o'clock on Friday evening the 20th of June, Joseph had a drink in the 'Fountain Inn', just a few hundred yards from where he lived. As he left the public house and began to cross the road he was struck by a bus travelling from Dixon's Green towards Dudley. He fell beneath the wheels and was killed instantly. He was buried in the grave in Lye cemetery with his wife Mary. Today, like Anabella Davies in Stourbridge Cemetery, there is no headstone or marker to indicate the place where the tragic figure of Joseph Dainty was finally laid to rest.

Nahid Akhtar, died 26th January 1978, aged 11 months

Like many towns in the Black Country, Lye has changed considerably over the past thirty to forty years. Not only has the appearance of the town changed but its newer inhabitants follow a very different faith to the old 'church or chapel' people of The Lye.

A photograph of the grave of Nahid Akhtar, who died in January 1978 aged eleven months, was among those taken many years ago by Denys Brooks but without any explanatory notes. Since that time there have been several Muslim burials in Lye cemetery which has a section specially designated for Muslim graves orientated towards Mecca. However, no Muslim burials were recorded prior to 1978 and it seems that Nahid Akhtar was probably the first Muslim to be buried in The Lye & Wollescote Cemetery and, as such, is very much a part of its history.

Chapter 9

THE CEMETERY TODAY

From its inauguration in 1876 until the formation of the Lye Urban District Council in 1897 (which became part of the Stourbridge Borough Council in 1933), The Lye & Wollescote Burial Board continued to be responsible for the interment of the dead of its parishes. During those years there were changes in the Board's membership but the aims remained constant: to maintain the upkeep of the cemetery and its buildings; to conduct the business of managing the cemetery – fixing fees and selling grave plots – and to provide an Arcadian setting for the remains of the dead. To that end the cemetery has been in continuous use for 130 years though, sadly, the cemetery chapels were closed in 1993. The intervening years have inevitably resulted in much deterioration to the building, particularly to the interior which was badly affected by a fire in the Anglican chapel, and the whole structure is constantly under threat from vandalism.

The West Midlands Historic Buildings Trust was consulted for advice on how to proceed to secure a future for the chapels. The Trust stated that in their opinion the building was of historical and local importance and recommended that an application for listing should be prepared and submitted. This was carried out and the building received Grade II listed status in March of 2005. In December of that year the Dudley Metropolitan Borough Council declared the building to be 'surplus to requirements' due mainly to the fact that the majority of services associated with burials at the cemetery took place at neighbouring chapels and churches. An Options Appraisal Scheme was carried out in 2006 on behalf of the West Midlands Historic Buildings Trust to investigate fully the potential uses for the cemetery chapels, and the Trust is now actively engaged in attempts to secure funding for the restoration of the chapels' building and putting them to a useful purpose.

In recent years there has been increased awareness and concern regarding public safety and the potential hazards of unstable monuments and gravestones. In 2007 the Bereavement Services department of Dudley MBC carried out an inspection of the memorials in the cemetery. Work was carried out on those headstones that could be secured safely in an upright position but, unfortunately, there were some that had to be dismantled and laid flat. Many of the original headstones and monuments no longer exist due to natural deterioration and, in more recent years, recurring vandalism. A permanent photographic record of all the present gravestones in the cemetery is being created by volunteers from Lye & Wollescote Historical Society.

From an architectural point of view, the preservation of nineteenth century cemeteries and their chapels is now widely recognised. With many of those created in Victorian times having now closed and their chapels demolished, The Lye & Wollescote Cemetery is fortunate in that it has survived intact and is an excellent example of the period. From an historical point of view, cemeteries are an invaluable record of the social history of a town providing a unique insight into its past events.

With the growth of interest in genealogy and family history, inscriptions on memorials are an important and irreplaceable source of biographical information. With more and more land being used for building purposes, cemeteries provide much-needed conservation areas with ideal habitats for plants and animals.

The cemetery today exudes an air of peace and tranquillity; a place for quiet reflection on times past, as was perhaps envisaged by those far-sighted members of the Burial Board who in 1876 took on the responsibility for creating a last sanctuary for the people of their community.

'Oh that my words were written! Oh that with an iron pen

and lead they were graven in the rock for ever!'

Job 19, v. 24

Appendix 1 - Cemetery Layout

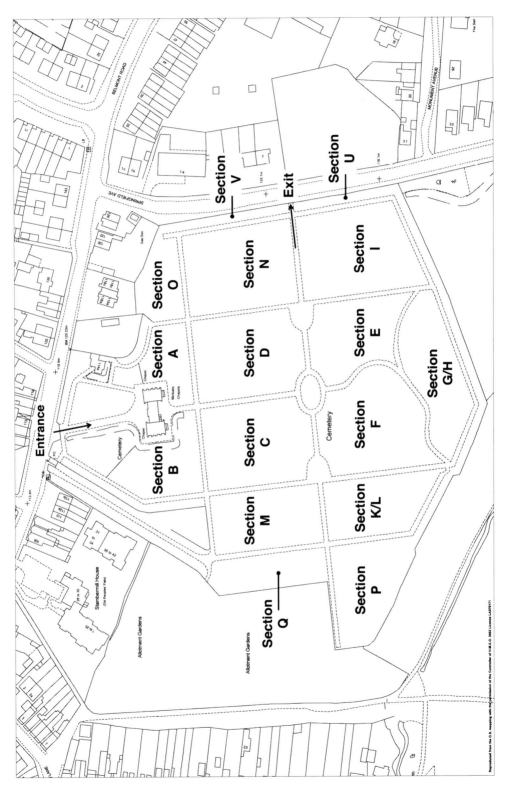

Appendix 2– Index to grave locations

KNOWLES, William	Section D 1R	Pg51
LAVENDER, Meshach	Section C 48H	Pg67
MILLWARD, Henry	Section D 18A	Pg30
MORRIS, Alfred	Section F 31	Pg45
NICHOLLS, William Ernest	Section N 48E	Pg34
PARDOE, Joseph	Section A 51A	Pg30
PARISH, Susannah	Section C 21R	Pg29
PEARSON, Hannah	Section D 19C	Pg46
PEARSON, John	Section D 45A	Pg20
PEARSON, Mary Ann	Section F 35O	Pg24
PEARSON, William	Section F 35U	Pg24
PEARSON, William Hugh Riley	Section D 4B	Pg50
PERKS, Alice	Section C 50S	Pg41
PERRINS, Amos	Section D 38A	Pg41
POWELL, David	Section K 10A	Pg25
RHODES, Thomas	Section A 54A	Pg37
RHODES, Thomas F.	Section D 48U	Pg46
ROBINSON, Thomas	Section E 1G	Pg17
ROUND, James	Section A 50O	Pg39
ROUND, Philip	Section A 52O	Pg39
TAYLOR, Alice	Section E 14R	Pg57
TAYLOR, Leah	Section A 52Q	Pg47
TAYLOR, Mercy	Section F 21F	Pg31
TURNER, Joseph	Section F 19A	Pg68
WAKEMAN, Benjamin	Section D 48K	Pg66
WEBB, Titus	Section D R40	Pg62
WEBSTER, Robert Thomas	Section C 48G	Pg48
WORTON, Joseph Thomas	Section D 50S	Pg32
WOOLDRIDGE, Alfred	Section O 20A	Pg44
WOOLDRIDGE, Henry	Section C 1A	Pg35

Appendix 3 – References and Bibliography

Original Sources

Dudley Archives & Local Studies:

Census Returns

The Lye & Wollescote Cemetery Burial Register

Newspapers:

Brierley Hill Advertiser

County Express

Dudley Herald

Worcester County Record Office:

The Lye & Wollescote Burial Board Minutes, 1876-1897

Bibliography

Bailey, B. *Churchyards of England and Wales,* 1987

Black Country Society, *The BlackCountryman,* 1995, 1996 Vols. 29

Birmingham & Midland Society for Genealogy & Heraldry,
    The Midland Ancestor Journal, March 1995

Brooks, D. & Dunn P. *Lye in Old Photographs,* 1997

English Heritage. *Paradise Preserved,* 2007

Haden, H.J. *Stourbridge Scene 1851-1951*

Palmer, R. *The Folklore of the Black Country,* 2007

Perrins, W. *Lye & Wollescote,* 1980

Perry, N. *History of Stourbridge,* 2001

Reuter, M. *Stourbridge & District in Old Postcards,* 1989

Rutherford, S. *The Victorian Cemetery,* 2008

West Midlands Historic Buildings Trust, *Historic Summary & Scheme,* 2005

Websites

The Lye & Wollescote Cemetery & Chapel Project:
    www.lyeandwollescote.info

The West Midlands Historical Buildings Trust:
    www.wmhbt.org.uk

The Lye & Wollescote Historical Society
    www.communigate.co.uk/bc/lwhs

Dudley MBC Genealogy Research Service:
    www.dudley.gov.uk/genealogy-research-service

English Heritage
    www.english-heritage.org.uk/

Index